11-04

MODERN WORLD NATIONS

MODERN WORLD NATIONS

Brazil

Harry Greenbaum

Series Consulting Editor
Charles F. Gritzner
South Dakota State University

CHELSEA HOUSE
PUBLISHERS

A Haights Cross Communications Company

Frontispiece: Flag of Brazil

Cover: Rio de Janeiro at sunset.

CHELSEA HOUSE PUBLISHERS

VP, NEW PRODUCT DEVELOPMENT Sally Cheney
DIRECTOR OF PRODUCTION Kim Shinners
CREATIVE MANAGER Takeshi Takahashi
MANUFACTURING MANAGER Diann Grasse

Staff for BRAZIL

EXECUTIVE EDITOR Lee Marcott
PRODUCTION EDITOR Jaimie Winkler
PICTURE RESEARCHER 21st Century Publishing and Communications, Inc.
COVER AND SERIES DESIGNER Takeshi Takahashi
LAYOUT 21st Century Publishing and Communications, Inc.

A Haights Cross Communications Company

http://www.chelseahouse.com

First Printing

1 3 5 7 9 8 6 4 2

Library of Congress Cataloging-in-Publication Data

Greenbaum, Harry, 1932–
  Brazil / Harry Greenbaum.
     p. cm.—(Modern world nations)
Includes index.
  ISBN 0-7910-7240-1
  1. Brazil—Juvenile literature. I. Title. II. Series.
F2508.5 .G73 2003
981—dc21

                                                    2002154356

Table of Contents

MODERN WORLD NATIONS

Brazil

Brazil is home not only to two of the world's largest cities, but also to some of the most beautiful beaches, such as the Trinidade beach and coast.

Introducing Brazil

Brazil is a giant by any measure. In area, it is larger than the United States without Alaska and Hawaii. It is home to the world's most vast expanse of tropical rain forest and to the planet's greatest river in terms of water volume. Among Western Hemisphere nations, its economy trails only that of the United States and continues to grow in strength. Two of the world's largest cities—São Paulo and Rio de Janeiro—also are Brazilian. Yet within the country's borders are some of the most remote places in the world. Brazil is home to more Portuguese speakers, black people, and Roman Catholics than any other land. The sprawling country occupies about one-half of South America, and it contains about half of the continent's population. Brazil is truly a land of superlatives!

Brazil has a very diverse population of more than 175 million people; within the Western Hemisphere, only the United States has more people. Its citizens span the cultural and racial spectrum. At one extreme, there are isolated Indian tribes whose way of life is similar to that of people who lived thousands of years ago. Some of these native peoples practice a culture that has remained relatively unchanged since before the arrival of Europeans. At the same time, Brazil also is home to many people who are well educated, speak several languages, participate in global activities, and are deeply involved in the challenges and opportunities of the twenty-first century.

Most of Brazil's early European settlers came from Portugal. Pedro Cabral, a Portuguese navigator, is considered the first European to reach the eastern South American shores that are now part of Brazil. He arrived in 1500, only eight years after Christopher Columbus's first landfall in the islands of the Caribbean Sea. The European settlement of Brazil, therefore, started many years before the British established Jamestown (now Virginia) in 1607. Many Brazilians take pride in the fact that they come from families who have lived in the country for nearly 500 years.

Before very long after Cabral's arrival, additional settlers began to come from a number of other places. Europeans from several countries flocked to Brazil, many eager to become involved in a growing plantation economy. Plantations needed workers who were able to toil in the hot, steaming, tropical climate, however. To fill this need, millions of slaves were brought to Brazil from Africa. The arrival of Africans helped start a trend toward ethnic diversity that continues even today. More recently, Brazil has received large numbers of immigrants from Asian countries. Many Japanese, for example, came to Brazil during the twentieth century. They have made valuable contributions to the Brazilian economy.

Brazilians are a friendly, fun-loving, family-oriented people. The distinctive rhythms of Brazilian music have captivated the hearts of music lovers throughout the world. Brazilians place a high value on getting along with people and

Brazil, the largest country in South America, is bigger than the United States, without the states of Alaska and Hawaii. The relative size of the two nations can be seen on this map.

are generally tolerant of others. Few countries in the world, in fact, can match Brazil's racial and religious harmony. Unfortunately, however, as is true of many other developing countries, Brazil has a much bigger gap in income and wealth than is the case in nations with more advanced economies. This is a problem that has plagued Brazilian society since the beginning; today, it is one of the major challenges that face the country's people and government.

During the nearly 500 years since European settlement, there has been much intermarriage among the races. Today, more than 40 percent of the population is of mixed racial backgrounds that may include combinations of European, African, American Indian, and other ethnic influences. In Brazil, skin color alone is no barrier to success, even though Brazil was once a country of masters and slaves. Blacks, as a group, tend to be poorer than other Brazilians because they started off as slaves and, even after emancipation (freedom from slavery), they often had to perform unpleasant tasks for very low wages. Only recently have educational opportunities become available for many blacks. The descendants of former white European leaders have long resisted giving up their traditional positions of authority.

Many Brazilians are unhappy that their country is making such slow progress in overcoming the rigid socioeconomic class structure that began with its colonial roots. There is, however, a saying in Brazil that "money whitens." This means that if a descendant of a former slave is able to move up the social ladder to acquire education, wealth, power, and success, he or she is readily accepted into Brazilian society. Important changes are beginning to take place in Brazil's social structure. Of greatest importance, perhaps, is a growing middle class. There is also a close relationship between increased opportunities and economic progress. The regions of Brazil that provide the best vocational and educational opportunities for poor people also have the highest rate of economic growth.

As a New World country, Brazil has a lot in common with the United States. There are, however, many differences as well. Some are environmental, since the United States is located primarily in the temperate mid-latitudes and Brazil mainly in the tropics. To know a country, one must understand its people and their actions. History, too, is extremely important to peoples and countries. A nation's position on the global scene and the well-being of its people are determined by political stability, good government, and a strong economy. Brazilians, like others throughout the world, look to the future with hope for their huge land, which is rich in people and resources.

Rio de Janeiro's unique Sugar Loaf Mountain is one of the best-known geographical features in the world.

Natural Landscapes

Brazil is a sprawling giant. Its area of some 3.3 million square miles (8.5 million square kilometers) occupies roughly one-half of the South American continent. In the Western Hemisphere, only Canada and the United States are larger. Of South America's 13 countries, Brazil shares a common border with all but Ecuador and Chile. If Brazil were to be superimposed over the United States and neighboring countries (area, not latitude), Brazil would stretch from the Atlantic Ocean to the Pacific and from central Mexico well into central Canada. Great differences exist, however, between Brazil and those North American lands. Most of Brazil falls within tropical latitudes. Only the southern tip of the country is within the temperate mid-latitudes. Its southernmost point falls at roughly the same latitude as Savannah, Georgia.

Within such a large area, one might expect to find great environmental diversity. Brazil, however, does not have the variety of features, conditions, and landscapes found in the United States. Most of the country, for example, has a hot, humid, and in much of its area quite monotonous climate. This has led people of European and African descent to avoid the vast interior. Throughout most of Brazil's history, the region remained isolated simply because few people wanted to go there. Brazilians were a coastal people until the last half of the twentieth century, with only a few exceptions. Even in the present day, some two-thirds of the country's area is home to only about 10 percent of its people.

Today, much more so than at any time past, all of the country's lands are being settled and developed economically. As this happens, many old myths are dashed as others are found to be true. There are many problems associated with development, some of which can have an impact that reaches far beyond the borders of this fascinating land.

LAND AND WATER FEATURES

Two landform provinces dominate nearly all of Brazil. They are the Brazilian Highlands and the Amazon Basin. Less than 10 percent of the country falls within other areas. A portion of far northern Brazil is reached by the southern edge of the Guiana Highlands, and the lowland plain formed by the upper drainage of the Paraguay River occupies a small part of south-central Brazil. Both areas are very remote and support little settlement or economic activity.

Brazilian Highlands

The highlands include nearly all of Brazil south of the Amazon Basin, extending from the Atlantic Coast almost to the western border. It is a region characterized by gently rolling or hilly landscapes with a few relatively low mountains. The country's highest elevation, Pico da Bandeira,

Because of its huge area, the geography and climate of Brazil's land varies greatly from region to region. This map's shading shows how the nation's landscape is more mountainous in the east and is lower in elevation in the north and west, where there are many rivers.

found a short distance to the northeast of Rio de Janeiro, rises only to 9,482 feet (2,890 meters). In many areas of the Highlands, streams have cut deep valleys, some of which have been dammed to provide Brazil with much-needed hydro-electric energy. The largest such facility is the Tucurui Dam, located on the Tocantines River south of Belem.

The Highlands reach their greatest elevation in the east, just behind the narrow ribbon of coastal plain, where most of Brazil's early European settlement occurred. Here, rich alluvial soils, tropical temperatures, and ample rainfall were ideally suited to the growing of sugar cane. It was the ability to raise this crop that first attracted the Portuguese to these shores. The Coastal Plain region is backed by a 1,000- to 4,500-foot (305- to 1,372-meter) natural wall that Brazilians call the Great Escarpment (cliff). This steep and rugged barrier proved to be a formidable deterrent to inland movement.

Inland, northward and westward of the highlands, the elevated landscape gradually dips toward the low-lying Amazon Plain. Many rivers begin in the Highlands near the coast, yet flow away from the Atlantic Ocean, eventu-ally draining in a northward direction into the Amazon River or Amazon Plain. In the south, some streams flow into the Paraná-Paraguay system that ultimately reaches the Rio de la Plata near Buenos Aires, Argentina. As rivers cascade from the Highlands toward the sea, many water-falls are formed. The most spectacular are the Iguaçú Falls, located between Brazil and Argentina near their border with Paraguay.

Areas of higher elevation in the east enjoy temperatures some 10°F (-12°C) cooler than the Coastal Plain. The more comfortable climate and the presence of vast stores of gold, iron, gemstones, and many other minerals combined to attract early settlers to a small area of the Highlands located inland from Rio de Janeiro in what is now the state of Minas Gerais.

Amazon Basin

The Amazon Basin is one of the world's largest, most mysterious, least known, least settled, yet most rapidly developing regions. It is an area of superlatives, home to the world's largest river (in terms of discharge) and largest tropical rain forest. It also is a region of untapped—and still unknown—wealth. Even so, the basin, which occupies roughly the northern half of Brazil, is a fragile environment where settlement and development must proceed with great caution.

Scientists identify not one, but three "basins" when speaking of Amazonia, or the Amazon Basin. First is the drainage basin—the area drained by the Amazon River and its many tributaries. Viewed as a drainage region, the basin extends high into the towering mountains of Bolivia, Peru, Ecuador, Colombia, and Venezuela, and covers an area slightly in excess of 3 million square miles (7.8 million square kilometers; roughly the area of the 48 American states).

A second way of defining the basin is by geological structure. Much of Amazonia makes up a huge geosyncline, a shallow U-shaped basin. Measured this way, the region stretches east-west some 2,000 miles (3,200 kilometers) and runs from 200 to 800 miles (320 to 1,300 kilometers) in a north-south direction. In this way, it covers an area of roughly 2 million square miles (5.2 million square kilometers; the size of the United States west of the Mississippi River).

Finally, there is the flood plain, or area that in geological time has been flooded frequently by the great river and its tributaries. Here, rich alluvium (stream-deposited silt) has been deposited to great depths. The flood plain covers about one million square miles (2.6 million square kilometers; comparable to the United States east of the Mississippi).

Because of the dense tropical forest, the oppressive heat and humidity, and the thousands of streams that form a barrier to ground travel, the Amazon Basin has revealed its secrets very slowly. Apart from the Amazon itself and its major navigable tributaries, until quite recently little has been known about most of the region.

The Amazon River is one of Earth's most amazing natural features. Its volume is unsurpassed, being four times greater than the second-ranking Congo of Africa and nearly 10 times greater than the Mississippi. Seven of the Amazon's tributaries are more than 1,000 miles (1,600 kilometers) long. In some places, the river is so wide that a person standing on one shore cannot see the opposite shore. Where the river narrows, water may flow 300 feet (90 meters) deep. At its mouth, the river's estuary is 150 miles (240 kilometers) across. Oceangoing ships can navigate the river some 1,900 miles (3,060 kilometers) upstream to Iquitos, a port in eastern Peru.

Paradoxically, the world's greatest inland river network has been of little importance. Population density in the Amazon Basin, until recent years, was less than one person per square mile (two per kilometer). It was home only to small and scattered populations of native American Indians and a few adventurers who sought their fortunes in the Brazilian interior. No major cities were built along the river's shores or at its mouth. The rich soils were of little value to farming peoples because the lands along the Amazon flooded not once, but twice, each year. Since the 1960s, these traditions have begun to change and the Amazon Basin has become a beehive of activity.

CLIMATES AND ECOSYSTEMS

Most of Brazil lies within tropical latitudes. Location on or near the equator, differences in elevation, and prevailing wind systems are the three main factors that control weather (daily changes) and climate (long-term averages). Climate is the most important aspect of a region's ecosystem—its vegetation, animal life, and soils. When most people think of Brazil, steaming tropical rain forests come to mind. Although the country is, in fact, home to the world's largest area of rain forest vegetation, Brazil also has vast areas of savanna and prairie grasslands, temperate forests, and desert scrublands.

Humid Tropics And Tropical Rain Forest

Roughly the northern half of Brazil—that area occupied by the Amazon Basin—has a hot, wet, monotonous climate. This is the world's largest expanse of humid tropical climate. Temperatures vary little from day to day and season to season. This is the world's least changing climate. Daytime highs in the upper 80s or low 90s°F (27 to 32°C) and nighttime lows in the 70s°F (lows 20s°C) contribute to averages that hover around 79 to 81°F (26.1 to 27.2°C) for most locations. It is often said that "nighttime is the winter of the tropics." This is because there is a much greater difference between the daytime high and low temperatures than there is between the average temperature of the coldest and warmest months. The tropics experience the highest average annual temperatures, but not the highest extremes. In fact, temperatures rarely if ever rise above 100°F (38°C). As temperatures begin to warm, clouds form to create a "shield" that blocks incoming solar radiation. Highest extreme temperatures always occur in arid desert regions that have little cloud cover rather than in more heavily forested places such as Brazil.

There is no long period of drought in the humid tropics. With few exceptions, rainfall amounts average 70 to 90 inches (178 to 229 centimeters) per year. Rain falls almost daily. Most precipitation comes in the form of thundershowers, which are often torrential. In places along the coast, where the Great Escarpment rises sharply to meet the moisture-packed trade winds that blow in from the Atlantic, up to 140 inches (356 centimeters) of rain may fall each year.

Constantly high temperatures and evenly distributed moisture help foster the growth of the world's most lush natural vegetation—the tropical rain forest, or *selva*, as it is called in Brazil. It is estimated that more than half of Earth's known (and

Although the rain forest is not an impenetrable jungle, as many people believe, it is one of the most lush and humid places on Earth. Many of the trees tower to such heights that they form a canopy preventing sunlight from reaching the forest floor.

perhaps as yet unknown) species inhabit the Amazon Basin. The rain forest is the world's most dense, diverse, and unique ecosystem. Hundreds of different tree species may be found growing within one square mile (two square kilometers). Most of the trees are broadleaf evergreens. In the absence of changes in sunlight, temperature, or moisture, there is nothing to trigger the seasonal falling of leaves. A single tree, therefore, may be in all stages of the mid-latitude annual cycle of change, at one time.

Some trees rise to more than 200 feet (60 meters), forming a dense, towering canopy of foliage that blocks out all sunlight. Above the forest floor, on the trunks, branches, and crowns of the trees, millions of other plants make their homes. In the absence of direct sunlight, though, the forest floor is relatively open and clear. This means that the rain forest is in no way a jungle, as people often believe. A jungle is defined as "dense, tangled vegetation." This condition occurs in less than one percent of all rain forest. In spots where sunlight does reach the forest floor, along streams, roads, or clearings, for example, true jungle can be found. Another myth about the rain forest is that one can swing from place to place on vines that hang down from trees. In reality, vines grow from the ground—where they are anchored—toward the tree crowns, seeking sunlight.

Because of the profuse growth of rain forest vegetation, people—including many scientists—long believed that the soils of the tropics were extremely fertile. Actually, they are among the least fertile of all soils. While the rain forest is growing, trees recycle soil nutrients. Once the forest is cut away, however, this process stops. Leaching (the washing away of nutrients by heavy amounts of rain) and organic decay in the hot, humid tropical environment soon rob the soil of its nutrients. Within a very short period of several years, the soil is worthless. Under extreme conditions, it turns brick red and hard, and is totally ruined. The infertility of most tropical soils has limited the spread of agriculture throughout much of the Amazon Basin and the humid tropical region. Plantation and other forms of farming have thrived only where rich, water-deposited, alluvial soils occur, as along the coastal plain.

Few animals inhabit the rain forest environment. The largest land animal is the strange-looking tapir, which grows to the size of a large hog. Almost everywhere there are also monkeys and rodents, including the capybara, which can grow to four feet (1.2 meters) in length and weigh up to 100 pounds (45 kilograms). Less common are large anteaters, the giant armadillo, and peccaries, or wild hogs. Occasionally, a moss-covered tree sloth may be seen hanging upside down from the branch of a tree. Jaguars and ocelots are occasionally heard, but rarely seen. The rain forest teems with insects, birds, and bats—as well as snakes, some of which are deadly venomous, some crushing constrictors, and some completely harmless. Most animal life is found in the rivers. There, literally thousands of kinds of fish, eels, snakes, turtles, caiman (an alligator-like animal), and other life-forms can be found. Some, such as the piranha with its razor-sharp teeth, the electric eel, and the anaconda (boa constrictor), can be extremely dangerous. For most people living along the shore, however, the Amazon's rivers are mainly a rich source of food.

Wet And Dry Tropics And Tropical Savanna

North and south of the wet tropics is a region that has sharp seasonal patterns in terms of rainfall. This is the condition that occurs throughout much of the Brazilian Highland region. During the summer, wet tropical conditions prevail. Temperatures are hot, humidity is high, and rain falls almost daily. During the winter months, however, dry mid-latitude conditions are the norm. Weeks, or even months, may pass with few clouds and little, if any, rainfall. Temperatures here are both higher in the summer and lower in the winter than in the humid tropics. Frost occurs only at high elevations.

Savanna, called *campos* in Brazil, varies in composition. Under typical conditions it is characterized by tall grasses and

The Amazon rain forest has an extremely diverse ecosystem that is home to many unusual animals, including this young tapir.

scattered trees. Many scientists believe that fires caused by humans are the chief agents responsible for the creation of savannas. During the wet season, plant life thrives. During the period of several months that sees little rain, the vegetation becomes coarse and tinder dry. For centuries, the native peoples and then the Europeans deliberately burned the land to clear it for grazing or farming. This repeated burning, it is believed, favored the vast open expanses of grasslands, many of which are used today for the grazing of livestock.

Other Climates And Ecosystems

Northeast Brazil is a region of arid to semiarid climate and dense population. It is one of the country's major problem areas, because of its frequent droughts, occasional severe flooding, and the extreme poverty of its people. Moisture-carrying winds blowing in off the Atlantic are blocked by the Great Escarpment, leaving the leeward (downwind) side of the escarpment dry. Rainfall varies from 10 to 25 inches (25 to 64 centimeters) per year, but in the hot climate, evaporation causes a great deal of water loss. Vegetation cover is limited to drought-resistant scrubby trees, brush, and shrubs. This is a hardscrabble land that has been devastated by four centuries of human settlement, farming, grazing, and deforestation.

Only southern Brazil, south of the Tropic of Capricorn (23½° south latitude), enjoys a mid-latitude climate. Here, conditions are much like those in the southeastern United States. Precipitation adequate for farming falls throughout the year. Summers are warm to hot and winters are cool, but not often cold. Frost occurs occasionally and snow is rare, usually being limited to higher elevations. The region was originally densely forested, but much of the woodland was cleared for commercial use or for farmland. Many non-Portuguese European peoples were attracted to this region because of its excellent agricultural potential and its cool, pleasant temperatures.

MINERAL RESOURCES

Brazil has been blessed with many valuable mineral resources. It has huge deposits of iron ore and manganese. There are good reserves of tin, bauxite, and several other important metals. Gold has long lured fortune seekers, first to the eastern Highlands region in the area of present-day Minas Gerais, and more recently to many scattered areas within the Amazon Basin. Brazil is also a leading source of various kinds of gemstones.

What the country lacks is abundant fossil fuels. There is no coal and very little petroleum. Geologists are optimistic that petroleum and perhaps natural gas deposits will be discovered near the mouth of the Amazon River and perhaps elsewhere in the Amazon Basin. There are uranium deposits, but Brazil has turned to clean hydroelectric, rather than hazardous nuclear energy, as its chief source of power.

ENVIRONMENTAL ISSUES

Brazil faces a number of serious environmental issues, many of which are associated with recent attempts to develop the Amazon Basin. Of greatest concern to the global community is the ongoing destruction of the Amazon rain forest. Estimates vary, but it is believed that some 5 to 12 percent of the original rain forest cover has been lost in recent decades. Some studies, however, show that at least half of the disappearing Brazilian rain forest has already grown back. Regardless of which findings are accurate, it would be a terrible shame to lose this unique ecosystem. If the rain forest were lost, the consequences could have a global impact. The rain forest cleanses the atmosphere of impurities that lead to global warming. An estimated 50 percent of all plant and animal species, would be lost with the rain forest—a great tragedy. Up to 60 percent of all modern medicines come from plant or animal extracts. It is simply not known what potential cures may be hiding among the Amazonian flora or fauna; what is known is that, if the forest environment is destroyed, they, too, will be gone.

Other problems, perhaps smaller in scale, involve tropical soils and water quality. Tropical soils become infertile soon after the dense cover of vegetation is removed. When land-hungry peasants move into the rain forest with the dream of free land and an opportunity to raise crops, their dreams are soon dashed. Once cleared, not only is the protective forest cover gone, but soil can be eroded away easily.

Another growing problem relates to gold mining in the region. Mercury, which is used in the mining process, washes into the streams flowing into the Amazon in large quantities. Eventually, it enters fish which, in turn, are caught and eaten, causing deadly mercury poisoning in humans.

This rock painting in Januaria, Brazil was created after about 2800 B.C. Brazil is one of the oldest regions on Earth. It was also home to some of the first human cultures. In fact, some people believe that the first human beings in the Americas first arrived in Brazil.

Brazil
Through Time

B razil is an ancient land. Geologically, much of the country's upland region is composed of crystalline, pre-Cambrian rock of the Brazilian Shield that dates to more than half a billion years. Only a few other places on Earth are believed to be as old. The oldest archaeological evidence of early humans anywhere in the Americas has been discovered at Pedra Furada, in eastern Brazil. Some archaeologists question the site and doubt that humans lived in the Americas nearly 35,000 years ago. Others, however, believe that when human beings first set foot on American soil, they did so in what is now Brazil.

NATIVE CULTURES

South American archaeology (the study of ancient peoples) has long focused on the high civilizations that inhabited the

Central Andes and the adjoining Pacific coastal region. Only recently have archaeologists discovered that Brazil, too, was home to people who were very advanced in at least some respects. In fact, the earliest pottery ever found in either North or South America was discovered near the mouth of the Amazon River. Also along the lower Amazon, evidence has been found of very sophisticated farming cultures. By creating huge fertile plots of rich, black soil, these early peoples were able to feed huge populations. One of their cities, Tapajos, may have had a population of 400,000. This number is comparable to the Mexican Aztec capital of Tenochtitlán, which some scientists believe was the largest city in the world at that time.

When the Portuguese first arrived in Brazil in the early 1500s, native peoples numbered between one million and 11 million. These figures, however, are little more than a guess at best. Early Europeans rarely penetrated the interior of this vast, tropical, and—to them—inhospitable region. They had few ways to learn about, or count, the hundreds of indigenous (native) tribal groups of the interior. In all probability, some 2 million to 4 million American Indians lived in scattered settlements across an area roughly the size of the United States, not including Alaska and Hawaii. This would equal a population density of between one and two people per square mile (two to four per square kilometer), slightly greater than the density of the state of Alaska today.

Most early native peoples of the Brazilian Highlands hunted, fished, and gathered. The country's abundant plant and animal life provided a rich storehouse of food, fiber, and other raw materials essential for survival. Many tribes living along the coast and in the Amazon Basin farmed. Because tropical soils are not generally good farmlands, over several years, soil fertility runs out, and the field must be moved. As farm plots shifted from time to time, so did the peoples' villages. This type of farming is known as shifting cultivation.

Forestland is cleared and burned, leaving unburned stumps and tree trunks to litter the ground. Crops are scattered randomly amid the debris. Manioc, bananas, sweet potatoes, hot peppers, and perhaps other foods are grown for home use rather than sale. When the land is no longer productive, a new area of rain forest is cleared and the process begins anew. This kind of farming has taken a severe toll on the tropical rain forest of the region.

Only a small percentage of the Brazilian population is comprised of American Indians, perhaps no more than 300,000 people. During the period of slavery, many Indians were forced to serve as slaves, and some of them intermarried with both Portuguese settlers and African slaves. Today, some 230 tribal groups remain, including about a dozen that have only been discovered by outsiders during recent decades. Although Indian people reside in many parts of the country, most live in northern and central Brazil. Here, in the vast region covered by the Amazonian rain forest, tribal groups live in scattered settlements. To protect native populations and their lands, the Brazilian government has established more than 350 separate Indian reservations since 1988. These reservations cover about 11 percent of the country, an area that is almost as large as Bolivia.

In recent years, the interior of Brazil—particularly the Amazon Basin, which is home to most Indian peoples—has been opened to outside settlement and economic development. This has placed native people in conflict with non-Indian peoples and cultures. The results have often been disastrous. Native people have been displaced from their traditional lands. Thousands have died of newly introduced diseases to which they have no natural resistance; many others have been killed by lawless outsiders who coveted their land for mining gold and other minerals, farming or grazing livestock, or cutting timber, among other activities. Because of the great stress imposed by newcomers and the threatened loss of their culture, suicide is rampant within many tribes. How to deal with people who maintain a traditional way of life—even if they practice an ancient Stone Age culture—remains a critical and unresolved issue in twenty-first-century Brazil.

Brazilians are proud of the many contributions of the country's Indian people. Dugout canoes, called *jangadas,* that were used by the native people are still used in northeastern Brazil. The native population has also influenced the nation's language. Brazilian Portuguese differs from that spoken in Portugal, in part because of the infusion of Tupi Indian language patterns. More and more Brazilians are becoming interested in the preservation of their country's pre-European culture and tradition.

EUROPEAN SETTLEMENT

The word *Brazil* means "glowing ember." When early Portuguese navigators noticed a type of tree with reddish bark growing along the Brazilian coast, they were reminded of the glowing embers of a fire.

Nearly all of Latin America—that vast culture region that extends from the Mexico's border with the United States to the southern tip of South America—was claimed and settled by the Spanish. Portugal, however, claimed Brazil as its only New World colony. It became the largest and most important country in Latin America.

Portugal Discovers Brazil

In 1494, just two years after Columbus's first landfall in the Caribbean islands, representatives of Spain and Portugal met in the small Spanish town Tordesillas to divide the New World between the two countries. All of the land in the New World that was located up to 370 leagues (1,110 miles; 1,780 kilometers) west of the Cape Verde Islands (in the eastern Atlantic Ocean) was given to Portugal. The lands that were farther west were given to Spain. The treaty was sanctioned and supported by Pope Julius II in 1506.

Looking at a map, one can see that not only most of South America, but also the United States, Mexico, Central America, and the islands of the Caribbean, lie to the west of Brazil. Although Spain acquired rights to most of the Americas under the Treaty of Tordesillas, they were prevented from taking over the northern part of North America by the British and French, who claimed and settled most of what is now the United States and Canada.

In 1500, Portuguese navigator Pedro Álvares Cabral and his fleet of ships sailed westward from Portugal in the hope of finding a route to India and the riches of the Far East. They landed in what is now Brazil. The natives provided the Portuguese with timber, dyewood, and a variety of other local products. One of the ships brought these items back to Portugal. The rest of the fleet continued on in its unsuccessful attempt to find India by sailing westward.

First European Settlement

When the Portuguese sailed away from Brazil, they left behind two convicts. They did this in order to establish what became the foundation of Portuguese activity in their newly acquired land. Early European settlers learned the local languages and mingled among and often married local native people. In this way, Portuguese and native societies (at least those from the coast) were bound together from the outset. From this humble beginning, the European newcomers began a process that melded a wide assortment of races, cultures, religions, and social practices.

Brazil's first permanent European settlement, São Vicente, was established in 1532. Soon after their arrival in tropical Brazil, the Portuguese decided that it was an ideal environment for growing sugar cane. This valuable product, which they had obtained during earlier travels in the Indian Ocean, became São Vicente's major crop. Plantation owners relied heavily upon Indian labor to grow their sugarcane. Indians also provided much of the food. Most of the Portuguese workers were male, and they often married local women. The settlement of São Vicente expanded rapidly. In 1554, a Catholic order, the Jesuits, established the village of São Paulo on the plateau above São Vicente. From this humble beginning as a religious center, São Paulo grew to become not only Brazil's largest city, but also the third-largest metropolitan area in the world.

Pattern Of Settlement

In order to help speed up the settlement of Brazil, the king of Portugal divided the country into large land grants. Grants were given to a small number of very politically important people. The individuals who held these grants were responsible for the costs associated with colonizing their property and financing their activities. They also had the right to pass on these estates to their descendants.

This pattern of settlement saved money for Portugal's rulers. It meant, however, that early Brazilian agriculture was based on the establishment of large estates, rather than the family farms that became the mainstay of agriculture in most of what is now the United States and Canada.

The Portuguese immigrants came from many different groups. They included the people who received the land grants and other rich individuals. They also included soldiers and workers who often intermarried with American Indians and later with African slaves. Among the Portuguese there was a sizable number of New Christians, people who had been forced by the government to convert to Catholicism. Many of them continued to practice Judaism and their other former faiths in secret.

As time went on, immigrants from many other countries arrived and easily mixed with the earlier settlers. They helped develop the present Brazilian society that is so tolerant and understanding. Despite this melting-pot background, Brazil developed a rather rigid class structure. This was influenced by the pattern of settlement that prevailed in colonial Brazil. Class discrimination is still a serious problem in the country. These class differences, which are often the result of unequal educational opportunities, have reduced the productivity of the poor. They are also a major factor in explaining the much lower per-capita national income in Brazil when compared to that of the United States or Canada.

A Slave Economy

Many Indians suffered after European colonization. Diseases to which the natives had no immunity killed many of the local people. This led the European settlers to import large numbers of slaves from Africa. The sugarcane and other export crops grown in Brazil required a large amount of manual labor. It has been estimated that more than 30,000 Africans were imported to Brazil during the sixteenth century. More than half a million slaves came during the seventeenth century. Over a period of about 350 years, an estimated 3 million to 4 million African slaves were brought to the country.

Slavery is a very cruel practice. Most of Brazil's slaves were taken from their homes in the Portuguese colonies of Africa. Families were separated and local cultures shattered. The slaves were transported across the Atlantic Ocean in a very inhumane manner, crowded into filthy ships with little food and water. After arriving in Brazil, they continued to receive very poor treatment. Compared with the slaveholders of many other countries, however, Brazilian slaveowners did not usually try to destroy African culture. They also did not engage in the type of racial discrimination that was prevalent in many other parts of the world. There was considerable social contact between those from African backgrounds and the other people of Brazil. Slavery was not outlawed in Brazil until the 1880s. When slavery ended in the United States in 1865, a number of American slaveholders purchased estates in Brazil and continued to use slaves to work the land.

Brazilians have adopted many African customs. Many contributions of the former African slaves still play an important role today. A large number of the traits and practices associated with contemporary Brazilian society—such as food, music, dances, festivals, and some religious customs—have been heavily influenced by the country's African cultural heritage.

Early growth

During the seventeenth century, Brazil experienced a rapid, but uneven, pattern of growth. With the help of quickly increasing slave labor, Brazil's sugar plantations expanded northward along the Atlantic coast. Most productive plantations and much of the population were soon located in the northeastern part of the country. Here, a tropical climate with ample rainfall and fertile alluvial soils that were washed down and deposited on the low-lying coastal plain, were ideally suited for the raising of the valuable sugarcane.

Brazil has generally had peaceful relations with the rest of the world. During the sixteenth and seventeenth century, however, both the French and the Dutch made many incursions into the country. After fierce fighting, most of the French settlements were eliminated by 1615. The Dutch were more successful, however. They occupied large parts of northeastern Brazil for about 30 years. The Dutch generally had good dealings with Portuguese planters during their stay in Brazil. They supplied the Portuguese with credit, imported goods, and European markets. They encouraged religious tolerance, and helped improve both the cities and rural structure of northeastern Brazil. Although the Dutch were forced out of Brazil in 1654, they continued to influence both

Brazilian commerce and the slave trade for many years. After they were expelled from Brazil, the Dutch started sugar plantations in other parts of the world. Their efficient system of production ultimately had a very negative impact on Brazil's sugar industry.

The Brazilian economy gradually diversified and moved in many new directions. Explorations into the interior of the country began to take place. Between 1693 and 1695, gold was discovered in an inland area located north of the state of São Paulo in what is now the state of Minas Gerais. A major gold rush took place, with thousands of people being attracted to Brazil and its newfound source of wealth. Additional gold discoveries were made in what are now the states of Goiás and Mato Grosso, and in a variety of other places as well. Much of the gold was found in mountainous and other hard-to-reach locations. Despite the fact that travel to many of the gold mines was difficult and dangerous, by 1760, the country was producing nearly one-half of the world's gold.

CHANGES IN THE ECONOMIC STRUCTURE

Brazil's cycle of growth has had many phases. Often, the country's economy depended heavily on a single item, such as sugar, gold, rubber, or coffee. This trend has contributed to a "boom-and-bust" economic roller-coaster. Periods of huge wealth have often been followed by eras of grinding poverty for the country and many of its people. Coffee became a major Brazilian crop in the 1820s, and the growing and shipping of coffee greatly helped spur the growth of inland São Paulo and its port city of Santos. Coffee remains an important crop today, although it contributes a much lower percentage of the country's wealth than it did in the past. In the 1880s, the Amazon region became an important area because of the increasing demand for rubber. Thousands of workers moved into the rain forest to tap the wild rubber

After they came to Brazil, the Portuguese quickly subdued the native people and forced them to work as slaves, cultivating crops such as sugar and rubber. This illustration, done in the mid-nineteenth century, shows native slaves growing coffee on a European-owned plantation.

trees. Since the 1920s, however, Brazil's income from rubber has sharply declined, because of the development of commercial rubber plantations in Southeast Asia. More recently, rubber production has suffered further losses because of the shift from natural to synthetic rubber.

During recent decades, Brazil has taken many steps to open its vast and previously isolated and undeveloped interior. Several highways now reach into and across the Amazon Basin. In 1966, the interior city of Manaus was established as a free port where shippers could trade without being taxed. Today, this once sleepy town located near the mouth of the

Rio Negro and Amazon has exploded to become a city with more than one million residents. In the 1960s, Brazil moved its capital from coastal Rio de Janeiro inland some 900 miles (1,448 kilometers) to a more remote site at Brasília—also a thriving city of more than one million people.

Meanwhile, the Brazilian economy has become much more diversified. Agriculture continues to be important, but the country is now an industrial giant as well. Service industries are beginning to expand at a rapid rate. Brazil looks to its past with pride and to its future with considerable optimism.

Brazil is known for its spectacular Carnival, held in the days before Lent each year. People of all classes spend vast amounts of time and money to make costumes and get ready for Carnival. Here, thousands of musicians and dancers are performing for an audience of about 100,000 people during Rio de Janeiro's 2002 Carnival celebration.

4

People
and Culture

Brazil provides an interesting blend of the customs and lifestyles of the many groups of people that have settled in this large and friendly country. It is also a nation of many contrasts. The Brazilian flag, for example, contains the slogan "*ordem e progresso,*" which means "order and progress." In reality, most Brazilians, who are highly individualistic, resent excessive order and are opposed to too many rules and regulations. They are also quite unhappy that more economic progress has not been made rapidly. Although the Brazilian national anthem refers to the nation as the "land of the future," yet most Brazilians actually place a greater emphasis on the present than the years to come. Brazil is a country from which much can be learned.

POPULATION

Brazil is home to approximately 175 million people. Only China, India, the United States, and Indonesia have higher populations. At one time, the country's population was expanding far more rapidly than its economy was growing. This caused widespread poverty and led to what many observers believed was severe overpopulation. Today, however, the country's rate of natural population increase (births over deaths) is 1.3 percent, identical to the world average. Clearly, Brazil's population growth is no longer a drag on the economy. In fact, if the country is able to better educate more of its people, its human resources will become a source of great strength and additional wealth.

Life expectancy has increased greatly during recent decades. Today, most Brazilians can expect to live about 70 years. Although this figure has been improving over the years, it still places Brazil near the bottom of Latin American countries in terms of average life span. Much must still be done to improve health care. Accidental deaths, including those resulting from violence, are quite high in Brazil. These factors, among others (for example, the country has South America's second-highest rate of HIV/AIDS), contribute to a 65-year life expectancy for males. This is the third-lowest on the continent, exceeded only by extremely poor Bolivia and tiny Guyana.

Settlement—the distribution of people across the land— is one of Brazil's most unique characteristics. The country's population density is just over 50 persons per square mile, but 81 percent of the people are classified as urban, or living in cities. This leaves only 19 percent of the people, roughly 33 million (about the population of the state of California), to occupy an area slightly greater than that of the 48 contiguous American states. Vast areas of Brazil remain relatively uninhabited, and therefore, underdeveloped.

In order to understand this distribution, one must look to history, physical geography, economic activity, culture, and perceptions. The Portuguese were a seafaring people whose settlements clung to the coast. They were accustomed to a mild and pleasant Mediterranean subtropical climate. Vegetation was scrub to woodland, with huge areas of park-like countryside and a farming landscape dominated by vineyards. It was their desire to grow a tropical crop—sugarcane—that lured them to the hot, humid coastal region of Brazil.

All of these elements contributed to Brazil's present-day distribution of people. Although tropical soils are generally infertile, the fertile alluvial soil found along Brazil's Atlantic Coast is a major exception to this rule. There, several important factors combined to create what was to become the country's pattern of settlement for more than 300 years. On the positive side, sugarcane flourished on the narrow coastal plain and the sea was never far away. On or near the coast, Brazil's early cities—Fortaleza, Recife, and Salvador, and farther south, Rio de Janeiro and São Paulo—were founded and grew.

Throughout much of its history, only the lure of a "rush" could draw settlers away from the coast. Gold, gemstones, and other mineral wealth drew waves of people several hundred miles inland, to what is now the state of Minas Gerais and its capital city of Belo Horizonte. Later, a rubber boom attracted fortune seekers into the steaming, remote rain forest region. For a short time, Manaus thrived as one of the world's most prosperous cities. Like previous rushes, this boom, too, was short-lived. Not until the latter half of the twentieth century did the Brazilian government begin to take strong steps to develop the interior and spread the country's population more evenly across the vast landscape.

A LINGUA PORTUGUESA
(THE PORTUGUESE LANGUAGE)

Portuguese is the second most widely spoken Romance language in the world (following Spanish). More than 150 million people in Brazil use Portuguese as their first language. Portuguese is also spoken in Portugal, in a number of African countries, and in many other places, including parts of India. The Portuguese language stems largely from Latin. It has, however, incorporated words from many other languages. A number of these words, such as *banana* and *batata* (the Portuguese word for "potato"), originated in the New World.

In colonial Brazil, the Portuguese language united plantation owners, slaves, miners, city dwellers, and members of the armed forces. It also helped distinguish Brazilians from their Spanish-speaking neighbors in South America. Although the Romance languages do sound rather romantic, the term *Romance* only means that they derive from the Latin language that was developed in Rome. Different dialects of Latin eventually emerged as separate languages. Aside from Portuguese and Spanish, other Romance languages include French, Italian, and Romanian.

The table below shows the numbers one through ten as they appear in different languages, showing the similarity between Latin and some of its offspring languages:

ENGLISH	LATIN	PORTUGUESE	SPANISH
one	unus	um	uno
two	duo	dois	dos
three	tres	tres	tres
four	quattuor	quatro	cuatro
five	quinque	cinco	cinco
six	sex	seis	seis
seven	septem	sete	siete
eight	octo	oito	ocho
nine	novem	nove	nueve
ten	decem	dez	diez

RELIGION AND CULTURE

Brazil is a country of many religions. Roman Catholicism is the dominant faith by a considerable margin. In fact, more Catholics live in Brazil than in any other country in the world. Brazil's religious framework has been influenced by a variety of traditions. Approximately 75 percent of the population says that they are Catholic. Even some Brazilian Catholics still incorporate a few African practices into their religion. Saints are very important to many Brazilian Catholics. In the interior of the country, a special reverence is often shown to Our Lady of Appearance, Brazil's patron saint.

Resistance to outside authority has also influenced religion in Brazil. Formalized religion plays a smaller role than it does in the United States. The position of the Catholic Church has also been hindered by its lack of success in recruiting priests. The shortage of priests is especially severe in rural areas. Church authorities are quite concerned over the fact that today only about one-fifth of all Catholics attend mass and participate in church activities on a regular basis.

The Brazilian Catholic Church leadership demonstrated considerable courage during the time the nation was governed by a military dictatorship. During the 1960s and 1970s, when military dictators restricted the freedom of the Brazilian people, many priests, bishops, and cardinals strongly and effectively protested against the human rights violations that were carried out by the government. The Catholic clergy further irritated the military leadership by speaking out to defend the rights of the poor.

In addition to Catholicism, Brazil has a great variety of Protestant denominations. It is also a home to Muslims, Jews, and an increasing number of Buddhists and members of other Far Eastern religions. There are also a wide variety of African and American Indian religions.

Membership in various Protestant denominations has shown an amazing expansion in Brazil. In 1960, approximately 3.7 percent of the population was Protestant. By 1991, the census estimated that 28.2 million, or approximately 19 percent of the country's people were Protestant. This growth was largely brought about through massive conversions. It has also been influenced by the immigration of many non-Catholics into Brazil during the last half-century. Foreign, mostly American, Protestant missionaries have been very active in Brazil. Their efforts have been directed most heavily at poor people in rural areas. Evangelical and Pentecostal missionary groups have been especially effective in winning converts.

During the period of the Inquisition several centuries ago, many Portuguese Jews fled to Brazil. Most members of this group have become assimilated and have intermarried over the years. They now consider themselves Catholic, but still take pride in the traditions and courage of their ancestors. These pioneer settlers differ from the present Jewish population that is comprised largely of people who have migrated to Brazil during the past 100 years.

Brazil has long been home to huge populations of various ethnic groups. For example, it has more people of at least partial African background than any other country in the world, including African nations. In addition, more people of Italian descent live in São Paulo, Brazil, than in any city other than Rome. All of these different peoples have shared their cultures over time. One very interesting blend of religion and other aspects of culture in Brazil is *Macumba*. The origins of this folk practice can be traced to the beliefs of early immigrants from Africa. It has also adopted many European traditions, though. Macumba incorporates spiritualism, folk culture, and formal religion. There are differences among ethnic groups and regions of the country in how it is practiced.

Activities associated with Macumba often include an outdoors ceremonial location, sacrifices, and many offerings. Mediums often assist in carrying out many functions and people often find themselves in a trance. Macumba involves attempts to communicate with holy spirits and it sometimes includes exotic dances and other movements.

Candomble is a form of Macumba that is largely carried out in the state of Bahia and places a heavy emphasis on the African background. *Umbanda,* another form of Macumba, is often practiced in urban areas and has been influenced by Hindu and

Candomble is a branch of the Macumba religion that focuses on its African heritage. These followers of the Candomble faith are dancing and singing in the streets of Rio as they carry offerings for Yemanja, the African god of the sea.

Buddhist traditions, as well as by Catholicism and African animist faiths. Many other types of Macumba continue to exist in various parts of Brazil, even though Christian churches discourage it. Despite the formal churches' disapproval, Christianity is often blended into most forms of Macumba. Use of the cross is widespread, and Catholic saints play an important role (though they are usually given African names).

SOCIETY

Brazilian society is extremely complex. Racial, ethnic, religious, and financial differences, to name but a few, could easily drive a wedge among the country's diverse peoples. Yet Brazil remains a land where such distinctions seem to be much less important than they are in many other countries.

Class Differences

To give a general description of people and cultures is quite difficult. In Brazil, there are many regional and class differences. Descendants of former plantation owners still hold immense social, political, and economic power. Former slaves, even in an environment of racial equality, are only moving up the ladder of success very slowly. In urban areas, change is much greater than in the country and rural villages. In the cities, higher levels of formal education, greater economic growth, and immigration have all brought about the rapid rise of a middle class.

A sizable part of the middle class is made up of people whose families came to Brazil during the past century. These recent immigrants have come from many countries in Europe, Asia, and elsewhere. Middle-class Brazilians tend to be hardworking. They place a heavy emphasis on education and on improving their quality of life. Members of the middle class have, therefore, made immense contributions to the progress of the country.

The growth of the urban middle class has also led to an explosion within the university system. Although the quality of Brazil's universities is excellent, many young Brazilians are earning their advanced degrees in other countries instead. This has forged stronger links between Brazil and the rest of the world. Such links have helped improve Brazil's industrial, commercial, and administrative status.

Social and economic progress in Brazil has been held up by the fact that those who hold the wealth and power are very contented with their position. Often, family connections and contacts have heavily influenced their success. In this kind of social environment, the type of innovative outlook—and willingness to take risks—that is associated with increased productivity and rapid economic growth is lacking.

The very poor, especially those living in rural areas, often feel that they have little opportunity to improve their lives. Many, however, have great respect for the people who hire them. By U.S. standards, wages are very low in Brazil, but employers often provide for their employees when they are sick or old.

Customs

Interpersonal relations are very important to Brazilians. They are warm people who readily show their emotions. Brazilians often hug and kiss their friends when they meet on the street. In some parts of the country, women give their married friends a kiss on each cheek. They give three kisses to their unmarried women friends—a practice considered an omen to guarantee the friend's future marriage. Showing affection to children is also an important custom. Complete strangers often kiss children when they meet for the first time.

Brazilians expect others to treat them in a friendly manner. Shaking hands is very common. People are often offended if an acquaintance does not offer a handshake. Fortunately for visitors, however, they are more tolerant of foreigners in this respect than they are of fellow Brazilians.

The distance or space considered appropriate between speakers often varies from culture to culture. The comfort zone among Brazilians is much narrower than it is among North Americans. In Brazil, it is not at all uncommon for a person to have his or her face only inches away when speaking to someone else. This closeness makes many people of northwest European (including Anglo-American) ancestry rather uneasy.

Interpersonal relations are also important in the business world. Business matters are not normally discussed until confidence is established between potential colleagues. The emphasis on good manners is much more pronounced than it is in the United States.

Brazilian society is not as punctual or as well organized as is the society in Anglo-America. When someone is invited to a party at 8:00, it would be considered quite impolite to arrive on time; he or she would be expected to arrive at 9:00 or even later.

Family

Family is very important to Brazilians, generally much more so than in the United States. The concept of family is often different from that in the United States as well. For example, Brazilian families tend to be quite large. Often, three or more generations live under one roof. Grandparents, aunts and uncles, and sometimes even more distant relatives play an important role in the Brazilian family-oriented society. Grandparents often help take care of young children while parents work to provide for their family. It is also customary for parents to live with their children when they are no longer able to care for themselves. Nursing homes are much less prevalent than they are in the United States.

Traditionally, men have dominated families in Brazil. The feminist movement, however, has begun to have an impact. Today, more women are entering professions that were previously open only to men. Two-income families are becoming much more common.

Community-based activities are less important in Brazil than they are in the United States. Many of the activities that are carried out by social organizations in the United States are conducted within the family in Brazil. Parties and festivals are often a multigenerational celebration. People of different ages mix with much greater ease than they do in the United States.

Peer pressure among Brazilian teenagers is not as influential, because of the large number of family-based social activities and stronger family support. Teenagers often engage in a wide variety of group activities. Young people get together on beaches, in cafés, in parks, and in homes. It is very common for families who can afford to do so to belong to private clubs, most of which have special activities for young people. There is very little athletic competition in

Brazilian schools. Private clubs, therefore, play an important role in providing sport activities for young people.

The Role Of Women

Brazilian social and economic progress has been restricted because the status of women has traditionally been inferior to that of men. Women were not permitted to vote until 1934. Divorce was not legal until 1977. In addition, educated upper- and middle-class women have generally been hired for professional jobs only during the past 30 years. The rights of women have improved substantially during the past three decades. Even so, their salaries and job opportunities still lag far behind those available to North American women.

Even today, there are distinct differences in how the sexes participate in society. Women tend to marry at a much earlier age than men do. Men, on the other hand, often delay marriage until they feel that they can support a wife and family.

Poor women have long been expected to work outside of their own family. They perform jobs such as house cleaning and cooking and sometimes act as nannies or serve in other domestic occupations. They are paid extremely low wages. They often live with the families that hire them in a very small bedroom. Nannies frequently develop a very close relationship with their employers and come to be considered part of the family by children.

Even many middle- and lower-middle-class families prefer to have outsiders do their housework, and those who cannot afford full-time housemaids hire part-time domestic help. Brazilian homes often lack many of the labor-saving devices common in American homes. Middle-class Brazilians also have a much greater dislike for manual labor than do most North Americans. Middle- and upper-class men and women alike tend to avoid physical labor whenever possible. Activities such as mowing lawns and other yard work that many North Americans take for granted are looked upon as degrading in

Brazil. Middle-class Brazilians feel that these activities should be performed by servants.

Upper-class women in Brazil live in luxury and leisure. Much of their time is devoted to shopping, socializing, and visiting the beauty salon. An expected part of their routine often involves hosting and attending many parties and festivals.

It is often much easier for a middle-class professional Brazilian woman to devote herself to an upper-level job than it is for a North American "super-mom." The Brazilian woman has the help of servants. She may also have the support of an extended family that lives in the same house or neighborhood.

Machismo still exists in Brazil. The continued dominance of men in society and business means that attractive young women are more likely to be hired than older women—even those who are better trained and have more experience. Personal appearance and clothing are very important. Plastic surgery is a flourishing business.

EDUCATION

Public education continues to be a serious problem in most of Brazil. Teachers' pay is very low. Class sizes are usually large; classes of 50 to 60 students are not unusual. Most people who can afford to do so send their children to private schools. Families often make great sacrifices to enable their children to get a good education.

Higher education is often free, or very inexpensive, from government-supported universities. Many public universities, however, have extremely difficult entrance examinations. Only those students who have attended expensive private schools stand a good chance of passing the tests and being admitted to a low-cost public university. Unlike many American colleges, Brazilian universities heavily stress classical and theoretical subjects. Courses that offer practical, applied knowledge and skills are often neglected.

Brazilian families take a strong interest in the success of

their children. It is customary for students to continue to live with their family while attending college. Students do not often hold part-time jobs.

Very few children from poor families are able to obtain a good education. Since students from different social classes go to different schools, the education system reinforces the social gaps that already exist between rich and poor. The resulting socioeconomic distinctions have hindered economic growth in Brazil and many other Latin American countries. As is true throughout most of Latin America, people from the upper and middle classes often try to avoid physical labor. Most poor people, on the other hand, lack the education needed to perform the tasks demanded as part of higher-paying jobs that require technical or academic training. The resulting waste of human resources has had a highly negative impact on labor productivity and Brazilian economic and social progress.

SOCCER

Soccer, which is called *futbol* throughout Latin America, is a sport of great importance to Brazilians. Soccer is played by Brazilians from all backgrounds. Poor people will even bind together socks and articles of clothing to improvise the soccer balls they cannot afford to buy. No matter where one travels in Brazil, there will be youngsters playing soccer—it is almost a national "religion."

The most famous, most liked, and most often-quoted person in Brazil is the former soccer star, Pelé (in professional soccer, Brazilians are called by a single name in order to make it difficult to distinguish among players from different backgrounds). Pelé was born in 1940 and played his first World Cup at the age of 17. He came from a very poor family and earned his fame through agility, cunning, dribbling, and scoring in both domestic and international soccer competitions. In his prime, he was one of the most skilled and widely respected athletes in the world. At the end of his career, he came to the

Brazil is the native land of Pelé, perhaps the best-known soccer star of all time. Seen here kicking the ball over his head in a 1968 game, Pelé remains one of Brazil's most respected and beloved citizens.

United States to promote soccer, which was just beginning to gain popularity. Today, Pelé continues to be involved with many charities, humanitarian activities, and other causes both in Brazil and around the world.

On June 30, 2002, Brazil beat Germany to win soccer's World Cup for an unprecedented fifth time. Ronaldo, Brazil's current soccer idol, scored both goals in the championship match. Winning the World Cup caused tremendous excitement among Brazilians. It helped elevate the sometimes depressed national esteem of the Brazilian people.

CARNIVAL

In addition to soccer, Brazil is world famous for its Carnival. This tradition dates back thousands of years. Ancient Egyptians used the occasion to celebrate the spring equinox, the fertility gods, agricultural revival, and a hope for rain. A form of Carnival also existed in early Rome. Slaves were freed, schools were closed, and wild parties were held. It was also a time to honor Saturn and other Roman gods. Early Christians objected both to the pagan nature and the many excesses associated with the earlier forms of the holiday. Pope Paul II made sure that many of the activities were tamed and that pagan customs were modified. Christian influence has also shifted the time of many Carnival celebrations. Most are now held just prior to the start of Lent.

Carnivals are held in many countries. They show little resemblance to the celebrations that were held in pre-Christian times. Their structure is continuing to adjust to the changes that are taking place in the living patterns of the different regions of the world. The event goes by many names. In New Orleans, it is called *Mardi Gras*, and in Germany, *Fasching*. Nowhere in the world, however, is a Carnival as important or as spectacular as in Brazil.

In Brazil, Carnival is more African than European. Many of the dances, costumes, and practices reflect the customs of a variety of African tribes and countries. American Indian cultures have also had an impact on the event. Brazilian Carnivals usually involve around-the-clock singing and dancing from the Saturday to midnight on the Tuesday before Lent. Carnival in Brazil is so well known that people in many other places, including San Francisco, use the Brazilian spelling, *Carnaval.*

Carnival is important to people in all parts of Brazil. In Bahia, Recife, and Rio de Janeiro, preparation for Carnival takes up much of the year. Carnival has many variations and often adopts the regional characteristics of the specific part of the country in which it is held.

Nowhere is the Carnival more elaborate or better known than in Rio de Janeiro. Here, the preparation of songs, floats, costumes, contests, and dances goes on year-round. The Rio Carnival attracts many thousands of visitors from all over the world every year. This world-renowned Carnival receives support from all segments of the city's population. It involves huge investments in time and money. Many organizations known as *escolas de samba* participate. They carefully plan and rehearse songs and dances, some of which they compose themselves. They also build elaborate floats. Contests are held and awards are given to the best performing escolas de samba. Poor people often devote a large portion of their time and income to purchase cloth and other materials and to design and sew their costumes.

MUSIC AND DANCE

Brazilian dances and music are famous throughout the world. Dancing, singing, and bands have a very important recreational role in Brazilian society. Music also has a strong impact on the social and political framework of the country.

During the military dictatorships of the 1960s, 1970s, and 1980s, many songs were written and sung to protest the excesses of the military government. Some musicians were sent to jail. Others, like Nara Leao, were so popular that military authorities were afraid to arrest them.

Samba (a dance) and *bossa nova* (a form of music) have been universally recognized as a reflection of the tropical splendor of Brazil. The origin of both samba and bossa nova comes from many parts of the world, a further indication of Brazil's rich and varied cultural tradition. Both have many variations, which often reflect regional differences within Brazil. They have been adopted for functions that range from carnivals to ballroom dancing.

Samba, which had existed in Brazil for some time, became famous in other countries during World War II. Carmen Miranda, a star of many Hollywood movies, contributed to its worldwide popularity. It is partially based on an earlier dance called *maxixe*, whose origin goes back to 1870. Samba skillfully integrates the beats of the polka and other European dances with the spectacular rhythms of the *batuque*, *maracatu*, and *sorongo* that were danced by African slaves during Brazil's colonial past.

Bossa nova, a type of jazz, was heavily influenced by samba. This famous Brazilian music, which did not come about until the 1950s, utilizes a quiet, simple rhythm that has captivated music lovers around the world. As a dance, the bossa nova is similar to the samba. The favored musical instruments for bossa nova are guitar, drum, and sometimes piano. Bossa nova has a lingering appeal. Many songs from 30 to 40 years ago are still popular today. These include favorites such as "Girl from Ipanema," "Bim Bom," "One Note Samba," "O Pato (The Duck)," and many others. Bossa nova has made many Brazilian singers, including Sergio Mendes, Antonio Carlos Jobim, Nara Leao, and Roberto Carlos, world famous. Many well-known American musicians, including Dave Brubeck, Frank Sinatra, and Stan Getz, also contributed to the success of the bossa nova.

CAPOEIRA

The African influence on Brazil can be seen in many other forms of Brazilian art. This is in part because African slaves retained their traditional pattern of life in Brazil much more strongly than they did in the United States.

Explaining *capoeira* is difficult. Slaves who had come from Angola introduced it to Brazil. It started as a form of foot fighting and modified over time to turn into a mixture of dancing, music, and self-defense. During the colonial period it emphasized activities ranging from resistance to enslavement, from a desire for cultural preservation to an expression of hope.

Capoeira places a very strong importance on flexibility and fast motion. Over the years, the structure of capoeira has undergone drastic changes. In its original form, capoeira was very dangerous. Dancers would swing their legs with sharp blades strapped to their ankles, sometimes only a very

Capoeira is an unusual mix of dance and martial arts that was strongly influenced by Brazil's African slaves. Here, two young men are performing the often dangerous capoeira.

short distance from the vital organs of their dancing partners. The early forms are now illegal and capoeira is now much safer. In its present form it is similar in some ways to tae kwon do. It still involves two people pretending to fight each other and making quick, graceful movements. Good coordination is required, as is much practice and good physical conditioning and endurance. Capoeira utilizes a musical instrument called the *berimbau*, which captures the rhythm and feeling of this unusual and exciting dance. The capoeira is now becoming a popular form of entertainment in many places outside of Brazil.

AMERICAN SOUTHERNERS IN BRAZIL

Immigrants to Brazil have come from many countries and for many reasons. Slavery continued in Brazil for 23 years longer than it did in the United States. After the Southern states were defeated in the American Civil War, some residents of the former Confederacy moved to Brazil. They established a number of settlements stretching from Santarém, located near the Amazon River and the equator, to the southeastern part of the country near the Tropic of Capricorn. They brought their families—and in some cases—their slaves.

One of these groups founded the city of Americana in the state of São Paulo. Over the years, Americana has lost most of its North American traditions. The city has had a very rapid population growth, and today, the descendants of the first North American immigrants make up only a small part of the population. People now speak Portuguese rather than English. Nevertheless, the city seal still retains the Stars and Bars that represented the Confederate States of America.

In October 2002, Brazilians elected Luiz Inacio Lula da Silva, a liberal politician who was once a union leader, to be the nation's president. He is seen here waving to a crowd of supporters just after his election.

5

Brazilian Government

B
razil has had many different kinds of government. In fact, since the country gained independence from Portugal in 1822, it has been organized under eight different constitutions. The first attempt to break away from Portuguese control occurred in 1789. Brazilian-born Joaquim José da Silva Xavier, popularly known as Tiradentes (the "Tooth Puller") led a revolution against the Portuguese. He was defeated and executed, but even today he remains a hero to the Brazilian people.

CONSTITUTIONAL MONARCHY

Brazil's march toward independence was helped by French Emperor Napoleon Bonaparte's invasion of Portugal. In 1807, the Portuguese royal family, fearing for its safety, fled to Brazil. Dom João, who soon became King João VI of Portugal, officially moved his country's governmental headquarters from Lisbon, Portugal, to Rio de Janeiro, Brazil, on March 7, 1808.

The king was well received by the people of Brazil. João VI made many concessions to them. For example, he eliminated the Portuguese monopoly on Brazilian trade and also ended many of the restrictions that had hindered nonagricultural manufacturing. In 1821, João VI returned to Portugal. His son, who stayed behind, was given authority to grant independence to Brazil, with the provision that he would take the crown himself. As a result of his rise to power, Brazil became one of the few Latin American countries that gained freedom without violence or bloodshed.

On September 7, 1822, the new leader claimed the title of Dom Pedro I and declared that Brazil was an independent country. The nation became a constitutional monarchy. Political participation by the people of Brazil was very limited. Brazil at this time can best be described as a plantation-based society that still relied heavily on slave labor.

In 1831, because of the many political problems that existed in Brazil, Dom Pedro I was forced to step down. In 1840, his son Dom Pedro II became king and a two-party political system was established. During the reign of Pedro II, Brazil underwent many changes. The population grew rapidly, as did nonagriculture-based industrial development. During this period, the nation also fought costly wars with Argentina, Uruguay, and Paraguay.

Dom Pedro II stayed in power throughout most of the 1880s. As Brazilian society began to change during his reign, however, it became clear that a new type of government was needed. Adding to the confusion were tensions among the military, the traditional landed aristocracy, a rising urban middle class, and coffee growers.

Another issue that divided the country was slavery. Against the wishes of many Brazilians, the practice had continued much longer than it did in most other countries. Slavery existed

After Brazil won its independence from Portugal in a bloodless revolution, Dom Pedro I declared himself the leader of a new constitutional monarchy.

in Brazil until 1888. Although the abolition of slavery angered some large landowners, by this time, most Brazilians favored the freeing of slaves. Ending slavery also enabled Brazil to modernize more quickly. Even so, it proved to be a difficult task to raise the standard of living of former slaves.

THE REPUBLIC

In 1889, Dom Pedro II was forced from the throne. Two years later, a constitution modeled after that of the United States was put into place. It provided for the separation of church and state and for free elections to choose both a president and congress. It also gave greater powers to state and local governments.

Brazil went through many changes over the next 40 years. Coffee became the country's leading export crop. Population growth became even more rapid, and urbanization continued to expand, especially in the southern and southeastern parts of the country. Like most of the rest of the world, Brazil was heavily influenced by the stock market crash of 1929. The resulting worldwide economic depression had a severe impact.

GETÚLIO VARGAS

In 1930, Getúlio Vargas lost the presidential election. Taking advantage of unstable political conditions, he led a revolt and overthrew the government. In 1934, a new constitution was enacted that gave greater power to the national government and extended voting rights to the general public. Troubles continued, however, and in 1937, Vargas eliminated political freedoms, closed congress, and served as dictator until 1945.

In 1942, during World War II, Brazil declared war against Nazi Germany and Italy and helped to defend the South Atlantic against Nazi submarines. Brazil also sent soldiers to help the Allied forces in Europe.

BACK TO DEMOCRACY

Democratic elections were held in 1945. General Eurico Gaspar Dutra, who had been supported by Vargas, won the election. Once again, a new constitution was written. Its objective was to protect democracy and to prevent another dictatorship from coming to power. The constitution again separated the branches of government, limited the term of office of the president, and gave more rights to state governments.

Despite the new constitution, this period of democracy lasted only until 1964. Vargas was elected in 1950 and took over in 1951. During his time in office, he diversified agriculture, reduced the country's need for imports, helped the working class, and enabled Brazil to cope with problems that had resulted from the Great Depression. Despite these successes, Vargas committed suicide in 1954. Juscelino Kubitschek served the remainder of Vargas's term. He was then elected to the presidency in his own right in 1955.

Kubitschek was responsible for the construction of Brasília. This new capital city was built in an isolated area located inland some 580 miles (930 kilometers) from Rio de Janeiro. Developing this very modern city was extremely expensive. Kubitschek believed that building Brasília would help develop the interior of the country and draw people to settle away from the densely populated coastal region. Today, Brazilians are still divided about whether this venture, which started a severe problem with inflation, was worth the cost. In slightly over four decades, Brasília has grown from a site of empty scrubland to a thriving capital city of more than 1.5 million people.

Janio Quadros, who was elected in 1960 in a hotly contested election, became the last democratically elected president before a military takeover of the government. He quickly became involved in several controversial activities. Most Brazilians were outraged over his attempt to ban the wearing of bikinis on the beaches. He also angered much of the Western world when he gave an award to Che Guevara, who represented the Communist government of Cuba. Quadros also faced much opposition in congress. He resigned after only six months in office.

Vice President João "Jango" Goulart, his replacement, also ran into troubles. Inflation was a major problem during his brief presidency. A divided congress also made it difficult for

Brazilian President Juscelino Kubitschek, seen here (at center) during a press conference in April 1960, was the driving force behind the creation of the new capital at Brasília. Kubitschek saw building the new capital as a way to foster the growth of the economy and population of Brazil's interior region.

him to win approval for his political programs. Goulart was considered too liberal by many in the government. On March 31, 1964, he was overthrown by a broad coalition of political and military opponents.

MILITARY DICTATORSHIP

Brazil fell under military rule, and a series of military leaders controlled the country for the next 21 years. Although military rule in Brazil was not as harsh as that of Argentina and Chile, many of the people's civil liberties were still curtailed and the power of congress was reduced. There were also a number of occasions when those who opposed the regime were tortured or murdered.

Over time, organized opposition to the military started to grow, especially among students, human rights advocates, members of the labor movement, and the Catholic Church. Eventually, the military agreed to move gradually toward establishing greater political freedom and individual rights. In 1985, the military allowed an indirect election, which—very unexpectedly—they lost.

BRAZIL SINCE 1985

Following the period of military rule, the 1985 election of Tancredo Neves caused much joy and celebration among Brazilians. Neves died before he could take office, however. José Sarne, who had been elected vice president, took over to become the first nonmilitary president to hold office since Goulart. Sarne's term started with rapid economic growth, followed by a period of severe inflation combined with huge domestic and international debts. The biggest achievement of his administration was the enactment of the constitution used today, which places a heavy emphasis on human rights.

In 1989, the first president elected under the new constitution was Collor de Mello. Mello, a former national karate champion, proved to be a poor leader. He was impeached in 1992. Itamar Franco, the vice president, took over. In 1993, a constitutional amendment was passed, reducing the length of the presidential term of office from five to four years. Fernando Henrique Cardoso, Franco's popular finance minister, won the 1994 election by a large margin.

In 1995, Cardoso took office. During his term, many things were accomplished. Brazilians greatly respected the way he handled the difficult economic, social, and political problems that Brazil was facing. His financial skills and achievements impressed many international agencies, including the International

Monetary Fund (IMF), which gave Brazil considerable help. Cardoso also made a great contribution by promoting, implementing, and reforming the 1988 constitution.

In spite of congress's great respect for Cardoso, and the fact that it changed the law to enable him to run for re-election in 1988, the executive and legislative branches continued to disagree about how to implement government reorganization. The separation of power, streamlining of government, reduction of corruption, and the protection of democracy is a very important issue to most Brazilians.

In October 2002, Brazil took yet another step toward possible political change. A former steelworker and union leader, Luiz Inacio Lula da Silva, was elected to the presidency on his fourth try. Many Brazilians, particularly those within the middle and upper classes have expressed deep concern over Lula's victory. Many consider him a radical, left-wing Socialist, and they worry about the future of the country's economy under his leadership. His election may also have an impact on Brazil's relationship with the United States. Lula has been very critical of President George W. Bush's proposal for a free-trade zone that would include all North and South American countries. Lula is also friendly with Cuba's Communist dictator (and the United States's traditional enemy), Fidel Castro.

BRAZIL'S GOVERNMENTAL STRUCTURE

The Federative Republic of Brazil, like the United States, has a federalist form of government. This means that the state and local governments, besides the national government, play an important role. Brazil is divided into 26 states and the federal district (Brasília), with states being further subdivided into more than 5,000 municipalities. The country has many regional differences, and government policies often vary widely from state to state. It is of great concern to the federal government to help the poorest parts of the country catch up to the wealthier regions.

The president of Brazil is elected directly by the people. Members of congress are chosen through a rather complicated system that is designed to protect the power of the many regions of the country. The congress's chamber of deputies has 513 members and the senate has 81.

Brazil also has a federal judiciary, which, like the court system in the United States, enjoys both independence and considerable power. In addition to the federal courts, there are separate state and municipal courts. Superior Court justices in Brazil, like Supreme Court justices in the United States, must be approved by congress.

The reorganization of Brazil's government is an ongoing project. Further improvements to the constitution of 1988 have been suggested. There are many differences of opinion about what kind of additional changes will be needed to make the government more effective. Deep divisions remain. The general public, the media, and political parties all have their own ideas about what is best for Brazil and its people. Brazilians are concerned about the country's skyrocketing crime, including some of the world's highest murder rates. They are worried about falling wages and a high rate of unemployment, both of which have contributed to the growing number of homeless people. There are a large number of controversial issues. They include welfare reform and taxes, the role of the military and the police, and a number of foreign policy questions.

It is still uncertain how effective Brazil will be in handling its many social and political problems. If the changes that have been made since 1988 are well implemented, Brazil may truly become the "Land of the Future."

Although Brazil has a great deal of valuable natural resources, many observers believe the Brazilian economy is not being developed to its full potential. Some industries, however, are thriving. Brazil's steelworkers, such as the men seen here, have helped make the nation one of the world's leading steel producers.

The Brazilian Economy

B razil is the fifth largest country in the world both in terms of area (3.3 million square miles; 8.55 million square kilometers) and population (175 million). Only Russia, Canada, China, and the United States have a larger land area, and only China, India, the United States, and Indonesia have more people. Brazil benefits from its great diversity of land features, climate, soils, natural vegetation, water resources, and mineral wealth. The country, which covers almost half of South America, is also blessed with a very large area of unrestricted domestic trade. Even so, Brazil's economy, in eleventh place among the world's countries, lags well behind its potential.

INDUSTRIAL GROWTH

In the past, Brazil relied largely on its natural environment and abundant natural resources. Its economy was heavily based on agricultural products such as sugar and coffee, on gathering wild rubber, and on mining its plentiful minerals. These unprocessed industrial products were exported, and the foreign income earned was used in large part to import manufactured products.

Brazil's road to industrialization, interestingly, got a boost from the Great Depression of the 1930s, when income from agricultural exports dropped drastically. The massive downturn in economic activity made it difficult for Brazil to export its agricultural commodities. As a result, Brazil lacked the foreign exchange it needed to import goods from other countries. The reduced supply of manufactured items from other countries caused the domestic prices of these products to increase drastically. The Vargas administration took advantage of this situation and initiated a program designed to accelerate industrial development. This policy was highly successful. Manufacturing and many related activities expanded rapidly in urban areas. A few years later, World War II helped Brazil expand its industrial production even more quickly.

Economic growth has continued at a swift pace since the 1930s. Brazil has become the eighth leading industrial power in the world. The country's economic advances have been helped by a rapidly growing population, increased urbanization, and a large industrial and financial infrastructure. Growth has also been facilitated by improvements in human skills, and in the nation's ability to attract large investments from other countries.

Unfortunately, however, Brazil's economic growth has not been steady. There have been periods of runaway inflation, when prices doubled every few months. There have also been economic slowdowns, during which widespread unemployment left many people so poor that they were forced to beg in the streets. There have also been complaints of excessive bureaucracy and there has been massive corruption among many government agencies and officials responsible for managing the Brazilian economy.

Brazil's economic success is extremely important to the rest of the world. When Argentina, Uruguay, and Chile experience economic problems, they arouse some sympathy and concern, but little worry for the progress of international commerce. When economic problems strike Brazil, however, they may have a domino effect on the entire world community. As a result, economic and governmental activities in Brazil are watched closely by the industrial world. Brazil's importance has encouraged international assistance both from individual countries and from international agencies.

International trade heavily influences Brazil's link to the rest of the world. Business firms from throughout the world are eager to export goods to Brazil. The many items imported to the nation are of great importance both to commercial enterprises and to individual consumers. In addition, the economic well-being of the world financial community is strongly affected by financial investments made in Brazil.

Many factors contribute to Brazil's often-changing economic structure. To understand the rapidly evolving economy, it is important to know about improvements in the skills and motivation of its people, changes in the efficiency and integrity of its government, and the support that the country is getting from the international community. It is also necessary to recognize the many regional differences that exist in Brazil.

REGIONS OF BRAZIL

Vast regional differences exist in Brazil. The country's settlement and economic growth and development have been far from uniform. There are also many cultural differences from region to region within the country. These contribute to widely ranging levels of education, skills, opportunities, and expectations among people living in the diverse regions of the country.

The northern part of the country is the most sparsely populated. It contains most of the Amazon Basin and nearly half of the nation's land area. It lags behind the rest of the country in both industrialization and transportation, and contains only about 7 percent of Brazil's population.

Southern and southeastern Brazil are the most economically developed. Most of the population lives here. This region has attracted many immigrants from Western and Northern Europe, in part because of its temperate climate. Most of the country's industrial production takes place here. It is also the chief producer of a large variety of agricultural products that range from corn, wheat, rice and soybeans to coffee, sugar, and oranges.

Northeastern Brazil, which contains well over 25 percent of the country's population, is also densely populated. The northeast is where plantation agriculture used to dominate, and large quantities of sugarcane are still produced here. This part of the country, however, suffers both from low income and from sharp income differences between the rich and the poor. It is also a region that faces constant droughts and other misfortunes.

Central-western Brazil, on the other hand, is sparsely populated. Brasília was constructed at the edge of this largely uninhabited region of the country to encourage the settlement of the nation's interior. Some progress is being made. Agriculture is expanding rapidly. The *Pantanal*, which is largely located in this region, is a haven for tourists who are eager to view the rich plant and animal life that abounds in the exotic virgin wilderness. The recent population and economic growth of this region has also stimulated improvements in roads and electrical service as well as telephones and other forms of communication.

In northeastern Brazil, agriculture is still the dominant industry. Many of the region's people are very poor, and they struggle to grow enough crops to survive financially. This man and woman are working to clear their fields after a terrible drought destroyed their crops.

GOVERNMENT AND THE ECONOMY

Between the 1930s and the 1990s, the government dominated many aspects, including ownership, control, and management, of the Brazilian economy. In the 1930s, the Vargas administration established many new Brazilian firms in order to decrease the country's dependence on imports and to create jobs for Brazilian workers.

As time went on, the Brazilian government put more and more new firms into business. Growth in private industry, however, was impeded by many strict regulations. They ranged from a rule requiring payments to fired workers (making labor efficiency all but impossible to achieve) to setting a maximum price that could be charged for goods and services. When private businesses failed, the government often took them over. It was also common for the Brazilian government to take part ownership of private domestic or foreign companies that were having trouble.

Despite government competition and regulations, private business expanded rapidly in Brazil. In some cases, the private sector was assisted by public agencies. The government, for example, established a number of national bureaus to help less developed regions of the country grow faster. One such agency was *SUDENE*, whose function was to speed up the development of the northeast. A similar agency was later set up to help develop the Amazon Basin. In addition, many state governments have started commissions to foster quicker economic development of their regions.

In order to stimulate private investment, the Brazilian government sometimes provided loans and tax incentives. At times, it helped domestic producers by restricting imports from other countries. The policies of the Brazilian government toward private investment have fluctuated widely as the government has gone through many changes since the 1930s.

Specific Enterprises

The Brazilian government established or acquired many industries, including commercial and military aviation, microelectronics, and electric generation. In order to reduce the dependence on imported energy, the government has been especially active in organizing numerous gigantic hydroelectric projects.

Petroleum had traditionally been one of Brazil's largest imports. To reduce its reliance on oil imports, in 1953 the Brazilian government established Petrobras, a government-owned monopoly intended to explore, develop, produce, and refine Brazil's petroleum resources. The agency succeeded in putting major petroleum fields to work, many of them off-shore. Brazil, however, still has potential for further expansion in petroleum. New oil fields in a number of areas, including the Amazon Basin, still await development.

The Brazilian government recognized that Petrobras was not as efficient in terms of technical skills and management as many of the major international petroleum companies. In order to increase efficiency, the government sold part of the company to private business firms during the 1990s. At the same time, it opened up the Brazilian petroleum market to limited private competition.

During the 1990s, the Brazilian government also initiated a policy of massive privatization in other sectors of the Brazilian economy. Among these were the steel industry and other manufacturing companies. This program also reduced government restrictions on many forms of business activity, ranging from financial institutions to agriculture.

Recent changes in agriculture have been especially dramatic. The reforms initiated in the 1990s included the redistribution of government lands to private individuals. These reforms have not only increased the efficiency of agriculture, but have also enabled formerly landless farm-workers to own their own farms.

Governmental reforms, better technology, improved transportation, and new marketing techniques have facilitated a reduction in both production and marketing costs. This has contributed to a doubling of soybean output and nearly a 50 percent increase in the yield of corn in less than ten years. Brazil is the world's leading producer of oranges, coffee, and cassava (used to make bread and tapioca). Agricultural exports

Sugar Loaf Mountain can be seen behind an oil-drilling platform owned by Brazil's Petrobas Company, the nation's leading oil producer. The government started Petrobas in the 1950s to develop the nation's natural resources. During the 1990s, however, the government sold parts of the company to private owners in the hope of making the petroleum business more efficient.

have again become very important. Consumers in all parts of the world increasingly favor the high-quality farm products of Brazil.

Nevertheless, there remain many uncertainties for Brazil's industrial and agricultural future. The nation's economic potential is immense. Its future, however, will be strongly influenced by the success of its government, by world economic conditions, by the ability of the private sector to exploit its new opportunities, and by the confidence of foreign investors in the Brazilian economy.

Despite its regions of untamed wilderness, Brazil is home to some heavily populated cities. Rio de Janeiro, is one of the nation's—and the world's—largest cities. This view shows the coast of Rio with its world-renowned beaches that attract tourists from all over the world.

7

Brazilian Cities

B razil has many cities, all of them unique. Each of the country's urban centers reflects one or more aspects of Brazil's rich history and diverse background. Cities range in size from the world's third-largest metropolitan center, São Paulo, to remote frontier communities that remain some of the world's most isolated urban settlements. The country's cities attract multitudes of visitors both from within the country and from the rest of the world. Older cities in the northern and northeastern parts of the country often show elements of Brazil's exotic colonial past. There are other Brazilian cities, however, whose flavor is very similar to the more modern urban centers of the United States.

Brazil's two largest cities are São Paulo and Rio de Janeiro. São Paulo is located on a plateau, which allows it to escape the very hot summers experienced along Brazil's tropical and subtropical coast. Rio's setting, on the other hand, reflects the natural beauty and tropical splendor of which fairy tales might be made. *Cariocas*, as the residents of Rio de Janeiro are called, are fun-loving, have many festivals, and enjoy the attractive surroundings for which Rio is world famous. *Paulistas*, who live in São Paulo, are known for their hard work as well as their industrial and commercial success. Both São Paulo and Rio have experienced very rapid population growth, as have many of Brazil's other cities.

Quite a few rural areas in Brazil lack both job opportunities and modern conveniences. Masses of people, many of them very poor, trek to large cities is search of jobs and better living conditions. In addition, Brazil's cities have been a magnet for immigrants from other countries. As a result, urban Brazil faces a major challenge in its need to train unskilled workers and create new jobs. In addition, city planners need to provide for new roads, schools, and hospitals. There is also a need for added police protection, among other public services. As is true in most developing countries, the many side effects brought about by very rapid urban growth are of great concern to Brazil. Another issue that springs up in the cities is a more personal one. Coping with the difficulties that are associated with life in urban areas also causes many social and psychological problems for people who formerly lived in small, often isolated, rural communities.

RIO DE JANEIRO

Rio de Janeiro is Brazil's leading tourist attraction. It is one of the most dazzling, attractive, and famous cities in the world. Within its limits lie world-renowned beaches, ridges, and mountains. Some of the city's world-famous beaches, such as *Ipanema* and *Copacabana*, have been referred to in songs, literature, and art. For people who desire a tranquil location,

Guanabara Bay, which is protected from the waves of the Atlantic Ocean, also provides excellent beaches.

Rio's attraction comes from many sources. It is the city of samba, Carnival, beaches, romance, and soccer. Celebrities from all over the world have come to Rio for weddings, honeymoons, and other celebrations. Rio is also a very politically active city that holds demonstrations in support of various causes.

Worldwide recognition has also been given to the beautiful women who relax along the city's pristine beaches. In addition, Rio's beaches are widely used for soccer, volleyball, and other sports and festivals on a year-round basis.

Sugar Loaf Mountain is one of the world's best known landform features. This giant dome, which is famous for its cable cars, separates the Atlantic Ocean from Guanabara Bay. Another landmark is *Corcovado*, or Hunchback Mountain. The well-known statue of Christ the Redeemer, erected on the crest of Corcovado, is a majestic monument. People on ships can see the peaks of both Sugar Loaf and Corcovado many miles from Rio de Janeiro. A trip to the top of either of these peaks provides a visitor with a spectacular panorama of Rio and much of the surrounding area, including Guanabara Bay. On a clear day, the city of Niterói, which lies across the bay, can also be seen.

Rio is a city of many contrasts. Tropical forests are often located just a few feet away from busy thoroughfares, residential areas, inland waterways, and the Atlantic Ocean. Both local residents and tourists wearing bathing suits can be seen on streets and beaches intermixed with people in business suits. To understand the flavor of Rio, it is important to keep in mind that, in addition to being a place known for fun, the city is also a major industrial, commercial, and governmental center.

Rio de Janeiro also has vast differences in income and architecture. The city boasts the beautiful and prestigious

Municipal Theater as one of its historic treasures. At the same time, nearly one-third of Rio's population lives in ugly *favelas*, or shantytowns. The primitive dwellings, usually found on hillsides, often sit right next to the luxurious homes of wealthy Brazilians. Many of the poor who live in these dilapidated buildings lack medical care, jobs, and education for their children. Under these conditions of extreme poverty, crime is widespread.

Rio, whose contacts with Europe date back to 1502, has enjoyed an exciting and rich history. Rapid growth of the city started at the beginning of the eighteenth century, when the port of Rio became the supply center for the gold fields of Minas Gerais. The influence and importance of the city was amplified by the fact that Rio became the capital of the Portuguese colony of Brazil in 1763. It also served as capital of the country from the time of independence in 1822 until 1960, when the government moved to the new city of Brasília. This controversial move was heavily challenged both by Brazilian governmental officials and foreign diplomats who were strongly opposed to leaving the beautiful environment of Rio de Janeiro. Even despite its loss of the capital, though, with a metropolitan population of more than 11 million, Rio continues to thrive.

SÃO PAULO

São Paulo is located on a plateau some 100 miles (160 kilometers) inland from the Atlantic Coast, and has a much cooler, drier climate than the coastal cities. It is Brazil's largest and most important city. Although not as attractive as Rio de Janeiro in terms of landscape, this sprawling city is Brazil's leading population center, with an estimated 18 million living in the metropolitan area. It also is the country's leader of industry, commerce, technology, and services. São Paulo is also famous for its museums, universities, architecture, and cultural activities.

São Paulo, seen here in an aerial view, is home to about 17 million people, making it Brazil's largest population center. Many of the city's residents are immigrants from nations all over the world. The diverse ethnic makeup of São Paulo's people has had a strong influence on the city's cultural flavor.

São Paulo's population is comprised of people who come from all regions of the world. Italy has provided more immigrants than any other country. The *Paulistas* also include large numbers of people whose ancestors originally came from Portugal, Africa, Germany, the Middle East, Spain, Eastern Europe, Japan, and other parts of the Far East. The city has also attracted millions of people from the rural areas of the state of São Paulo, and from other parts of Brazil as well. In Sao Paulo, one can find restaurants that serve *feijoada* (Brazilian black beans) and other traditional foods. Others serve genuine Neapolitan pizza and a wide variety of delicious Italian pastas. Pita bread and *kibbe* from the Middle East, Japanese and Chinese foods, and specialties from most other parts of the world can be readily obtained, too.

Perhaps the most appealing attribute of São Paulo is the ability of its diverse population to live together in harmony. Widespread intermarriage among the various nationalities and races has given São Paulo a very colorful racial heritage.

Extensive immigration to São Paulo over the last hundred years has influenced the city's social structure in other ways as well. Much of the rest of the country is heavily influenced by the traditions of colonial Brazil. In these areas, the majority of the population is generally either very rich or very poor. São Paulo, on the other hand, has developed a thriving middle class. This has greatly contributed to the city's commercial and industrial growth. São Paulo's people are better educated and better trained than many other Brazilians. They live in a more temperate climate that provides fewer temptations to abandon work for fun then do lush, tropical locations such as Rio de Janeiro. Somewhat smaller gaps in income, which make São Paulo more like cities in the United States, create an incentive for hard work and a desire for economic improvement.

The São Paulo Museum of Contemporary Art holds the most important modern art show in Latin America. The Butanta Institute Snake Farm, which is also located in São Paulo, produces serum used to treat snakebites. It also carries out extensive research. Among São Paulo's many other cultural attractions are its Municipal Theater and symphony orchestra.

The University of São Paulo and the city's other universities are world renowned. Because of its well-educated population, São Paulo is also famous for its excellent newspapers. Sports are also very important. Morumbi Stadium is one of the world's largest sports facilities, capable of holding 150,000 soccer fans. São Paulo also has facilities for activities that range from swimming to auto racing.

Despite its many good points, São Paulo has been described as an awkward giant. Established in 1554, the city had a population of only about 20,000 by 1840. Railroads, industrial development, and coffee production enabled São Paulo to become a city of nearly a quarter of a million people by 1900. Today, the population of metropolitan São Paulo is estimated to be in excess of 18 million people.

As the city grew, many beautiful homes, office buildings, private clubs, museums, theaters, and sport arenas were constructed. Still, São Paulo has suffered from a lack of urban planning. This has resulted in a helter-skelter pattern of development. Until 1972, there was no city zoning at all. The widening of streets, development of parks, improvement of public transportation, and the stimulation of urban growth is, therefore, a major challenge for São Paulo in the early twenty-first century.

RECIFE AND SALVADOR

Recife and Salvador are both located in northeastern Brazil. They differ from São Paulo in many ways. These cities still reflect the traditional lifestyles of colonial Brazil. The way of life is much slower in pace and the gaps in income between rich and poor are much greater than in São Paulo.

Many residents of this region trace their ancestry to the plantation era of Portuguese land ownership and African slave labor. An American Indian influence is also significant here. The attractive appearance of the residents of these cities displays the racial blending that has taken place over the years. In its early history, both French and British fleets attacked Recife. The Dutch occupied the city for 24 years during the seventeenth century. Nevertheless, it retains relatively little British, French, or Dutch influence.

Recife is the largest city in northeastern Brazil. Like Rio, it is located on the Atlantic Coast. The name *Recife* means "reefs." The city's reefs protect its beaches, which draw many tourists to Recife. The city's beauty has been enhanced by its many waterways and bridges. In fact, Recife is often referred to as the "Venice of Brazil."

Recife is known for the warmth of its people and its many cultural activities. Art, sculpture, and music are prevalent. Although Recife has its own symphony orchestra that performs classical music, a much greater emphasis is placed on music and dances with an African flavor.

The city is known for its many festivals. The celebrations begin two months before Carnival. Costume parties and dancing abound. The samba is very popular. So are many other dances, including the *frevo*, for which Recife is famous. Beach parties are a popular form of entertainment. The *Bumba-Meu-Boi,* a famous local pageant, and open-air plays are other unique Recife events.

Salvador is the capital of the state of Bahia. Although Salvador is its official name, the city, which is located along All Saints Bay, is often referred to as Bahia. It is one of the country's oldest cities. It served as capital of the Portuguese colony of Brazil until 1763.

Bahia, like Recife, has a strong African tradition. In its early history, Bahia was a major center for the Portuguese slave trade. The city is known for African music, spicy African cooking, and African religions, especially *candomble.* Bahia is also renowned for its old churches and other architectural treasures. Especially famous is the Church of the Convent of the Third Order of St. Francis and the Barra lighthouse. Bahia provides an interesting blend of its historic sixteenth-century past and twenty-first-century present.

Adding to the picturesque appearance of Bahia is the separation of the city into lower and upper sectors. The lower part of the city includes the port and surrounding areas, which are located at the foot of a cliff on a small strip of low land facing the bay. The majority of the city lies on the upper level. Connecting the two parts of the city are a few roads and a 234-foot (71-meter) elevator.

Bahia attracts many foreign and domestic tourists each year. The city is especially attractive to Brazilians from other parts of the nation, who are interested in their country's early colonial history.

BRASÍLIA

Brasília differs in many ways from the cities of the northeast. It lacks both the warmth and the tradition of the former colonial cities. Brasília, however, is very modern. Major components of the city were constructed in the record time of three years. In 1960, the Brazilian government began to move its offices from Rio into this distinctive new capital located deep within the country's eastern interior. The interesting layout of the city was designed by two Brazilians—urban planner Lúcio Costa and famous architect Oscar Niemeyer.

Adding to the distinct appearance of the city is an artificial lake that separates it from nearby areas. Brasília's is often thought to resemble a bird or airplane. There are wings on two sides and a body in the middle. The city also has some spectacular government buildings. The *Palacio do Itamaraty* contains beautiful arches, a reflecting pool, and lovely landscaping.

Some of Brasília's other attractions include many parks— one of which is also a sanctuary for endangered animals— a modern cathedral, and a memorial to President Juscelino

Unlike many capital cities around the world, Brasília was built in the twentieth century, and as a result, it has a distinctive modern look. Seen here is the sleek building in which the National Congress meets.

Kubitschek, without whose effort this unique capital would never have been built.

CITIES OF THE NORTH

In spite of the fact that northern Brazil is sparsely settled and has many uninhabited areas, this region does contain some major cities. The history, topography, transportation network, and occupational and industrial structure of most cities in this region are strongly influenced by the Amazon River.

This part of Brazil includes the states of Amazonas, Pará, Amapá, Tocantins, Roraima, Acre, and Rondônia. Among the more important cities are Belém, Boa Vista, Gurupi, Macapá,

Manaus, and Santarém. Two of the cities, Belém and Manaus, deserve special attention.

Belém

Belém, which means "Bethlehem" in Portuguese, is the capital of the state of Pará. It is located near the Bay of Marajo at the southern edge of the Amazon Delta. A major port, Belém is approximately 80 miles (130 kilometers) from the Atlantic Ocean. It is located almost on the equator and has a very hot, humid climate. Its annual rainfall is well over 80 inches (203 centimeters) a year, making it one of the wettest large cities of the world. Belém was founded in 1616. Although it is younger than Rio de Janeiro, São Paulo, Recife, or Bahia, Belém predates the 1620 arrival of the Pilgrims in the United States by four years.

Since its early history, Belém has exported items that were grown, extracted, or plundered from inland areas. The economic health of the city has alternated with the many ups and downs of the regional economy. Today, the export of the diverse crops produced in the Amazon Basin still has a major impact on Belém's economic structure. Manufacturing has been increasing in importance over the years. Even this aspect of the economy is heavily influenced by Belém's location. Agricultural processing, shipbuilding, and sawmills, for example, are among the city's most important industries.

The city of Belém is heavily influenced by its waterfront. Stretching along its banks is the Ver-O-Peso market. This site, which extends for a number of blocks, provides a good example of the kinds of food and clothing produced and consumed in the area. It also offers excellent insight into the culture and beliefs of the people. Among the items for sale are rings and necklaces that wearers hope will protect them from evil spirits.

Belém is an appealing city. It has charming tree-lined streets. The Emilio Goeidi Museum also serves as a research center. It offers a great deal of useful information about the history, people, plants, and animals of the Amazon Basin. Belem has many other significant landmarks, too. They include the Governor's Place, one of Brazil's largest historic cathedrals, and a well-known classical theater.

Manaus

A major international port, Manaus is located nearly 1,000 miles (1,610 kilometers) from the Atlantic Ocean. Actually, Manaus is situated several miles upstream on the Rio Negro, before its juncture with the larger Amazon. Oceangoing vessels from many countries navigate the Amazon River for the entire distance. This ocean-based commerce is aided by the dredging of the river. Shipping and commerce here are facilitated by floating docks that adjust to annual fluctuations in the river's water level that may rise to 90 feet (27 meters). River-based commerce through the use of ocean-going vessels may continue westward on the Amazon all the way to Iquitos, Peru.

This amazing city, like Belém, has been heavily influenced by changes in business activity in the Amazon Basin. The economy of the city prospered during the wild rubber boom of the late nineteenth century. During the rubber boom, many changes were made in the city. They included the construction of a magnificent opera house with a unique green and orange dome. During its period of prosperity, Manaus attracted many prestigious domestic and international entertainers who performed at the opera house. The city has also become well known for its botanical gardens and its anthropological museum. When the rubber economy declined, Manaus suffered greatly. The once-thriving city began to wither away.

The Amazon River has also had a very strong influence on Manaus's social, political, and cultural life. To many people, the city's main attraction is its location. The Amazon region provides a visitor to Manaus with the impact of an immense jungle, the world's most voluminous river, and many other interesting natural wonders, including the fearsome flesh-eating piranha fish.

CITIES OF THE SOUTH

The south of Brazil differs widely from the rest of the country. Compared with the rest of the country, southern Brazil has fewer slums and the middle class is much better developed. Much of southern Brazil also has a cooler and healthier climate than the rest of the country. The unique attributes of this part of the nation are reflected in the structure of its cities. European immigrants (from countries other than Portugal) have strongly influenced the lifestyle of this region. The nearby countries of Argentina and Uruguay have also had an impact.

In the Northern Hemisphere, as one goes farther north, the weather gets colder. The opposite is true in the Southern Hemisphere. Because most of Brazil is south of the equator, the southern part of the country is the coolest. The Tropic of Capricorn, which separates the tropical zone from the temperate climate zone, runs through northern Paraná. Therefore, almost all of the three southernmost states—Paraná, Santa Catarina, and Rio Grande do Sul—are not technically located in the tropics. Some of the higher elevations of southern Brazil even experience occasional snowfall. This sometimes attracts tourists from other parts of Brazil, who have never seen snow. The differences in climate have also influenced the makeup of the region's population. The cooler climate of this part of Brazil has lured many immigrants from Italy and Switzerland, as well as Germany, Poland, and other parts of Eastern Europe.

The foods of southern Brazil echo the background of its inhabitants. Traditional Brazilian foods such as rice and beans are not very popular. Instead, foods are heavily influenced by the dietary choices found in Italy and Central and Eastern Europe.

Agriculture is also different in southern Brazil. In part, this is due to the region's climate and soil, but also important is the fact that many of the settlers here came from small, individually owned farms rather than from large plantations. Italian settlers introduced many of the varieties of grapes that have made the vineyards of southern Brazil famous.

Rio Grande do Sul

Rio Grande do Sul is the most southern state in Brazil. Argentina and Uruguay, as well as the Brazilian state of Santa Catarina, border it. The neighboring countries have influenced Rio Grande do Sul in many ways. Large parts of southern Rio Grande do Sul have *pampas*, or prairies, that are very similar to those of Argentina.

Porto Alegre, which translates as "Happy Port," is the state's capital city. Porto Alegre is Brazil's sixth-largest city, and has enjoyed a very rapid rate of economic growth over the past century. The original settlers of Porto Alegre came from the Azores. Ever since the nineteenth century, however, the majority of the residents have been German and Italian.

Porto Alegre is proud of its strong financial, commercial, and industrial growth. The rich agricultural land that abounds in Rio Grande do Sul has helped the city flourish. Outstanding educational facilities have also contributed to the city's economic expansion. An excellent freshwater port and the region's very good highway, rail, and air connections have also aided the development of Porto Alegre's population and economy.

Porto Alegre's businesslike atmosphere and dynamic growth provides sharp contrast to the relaxed atmosphere common in northern and northeastern Brazil. Unlike Rio and the cities of the north, in Porto Alegre, tourism is not a major industry.

Santa Catarina

To the north of Rio Grande do Sul is Santa Catarina, which is probably the most typically European state in Brazil. Most of Florianópolis, the capital of Santa Catarina, is located on a large island. One of the longest bridges in the country links the two parts of the city—most residential areas are found on the island, whereas much of the industry is on the mainland.

Despite the fact that settlement of the region dates back to 1542, the city of Florianópolis is very modern. Much of its population is composed of people who have emigrated from Europe more recently. Florianópolis is an attractive city that is close to some of the exceptionally beautiful beaches for which this part of Santa Catarina is known.

Immigrants from Germany settled Blumenau, also located in the state of Santa Catarina, in the middle of the nineteenth century. The city has not lost its German flavor. Germans in Blumenau brag about having the largest *Octoberfest* (beer festival) outside of Germany. Textiles are a major industry in the city. A large amount of cotton is grown in surrounding areas.

Paraná

Curitiba is the capital of Paraná, which lies between the states of Santa Catarina and São Paulo. The coastal range of mountains that separates São Paulo from the nearby Atlantic Ocean also separates Curitiba from the ocean. Located over 3,000 feet (900 meters) above sea level, Curitiba enjoys a relatively cool climate. The Iguaçú River originates near Curitiba.

Going by train from Curitiba to the port of Paranagua is an interesting trip. For approximately 70 miles (113 kilometers), the descending train passes through many tunnels and bridges. Near the ocean the vegetation is lush, the climate is both warm and humid, and the background of the people is very different from what is found in Curitiba. Along the coast, many people are descendants of early settlers and American Indians.

Curitiba had fewer than 150,000 people in 1940. The present population of the metropolitan area is well over 2 million. Many residents are the descendants of German, Italian, and Polish immigrants. Employment opportunities have also attracted other people from both domestic and foreign places to the city.

Curitiba is a very modern industrial city, but it has managed to avoid much of the clutter and disorganization that has plagued São Paulo and numerous other cities that have also had extremely rapid growth. The city has provided parks, created new lakes, and established many other recreational facilities.

Iguaçú Falls

On the western border of Paraná lies an attraction that brings many thousands of visitors every year, Iguaçú Falls, one of the world's most spectacular natural wonders. The spectacular falls are located about 14 miles (23 kilometers) from the area where the Paraná and Iguaçú rivers meet. They also are situated at the juncture of the borders of Brazil, Argentina, and Paraguay. The Iguaçú Falls extend for approximately two miles (3.2 kilometers), making them wider than Africa's Victoria Falls. The more than 250 separate cataracts (waterfalls) are unequaled elsewhere in the world. The water's 235-foot (72-meter) plunge dwarfs the 167-foot (51-meter) vertical drop of Niagara Falls. Mist from the falls often rises 500 feet (150 meters) into the air, providing viewers with an impressive rainbow effect.

Both Brazil and Argentina have national parks on their respective sides of the falls. These parks preserve the wildlife, vegetation, and beauty of the region, while also adding to the enjoyment of tourists who visit this amazing two-country attraction.

At the point where the Paraná and Iguaçú rivers meet lies one of Brazil's most spectacular geographical features—Iguaçú Falls. These waterfalls are much larger than some of the world's most famous ones, including Niagara Falls at the U.S.-Canadian border and Victoria Falls in Zimbabwe, Africa.

It is easy to fall in love with Brazil. The country has a great deal to offer in terms of geographical beauty. It has a wealth of both natural and human resources. No matter where they live, its people are attractive, fun-loving, and hospitable. Adding to the splendor of this exciting country is the magnificence and diversity of its cities.

The outward-looking people of Brazil are interested in issues that touch the entire world. These students are releasing balloons to mark the International Day for AIDS in 1997. With its long heritage and its vision for the future, Brazil is a nation with limitless potential.

CHAPTER

8

Brazil Looks to the Future

B razil is a land with unlimited potential. It is a country of friendly people who cherish family relations. Brazil has also experienced rapid economic growth and made impressive progress in improving its educational and social structure in recent years. The country, nevertheless, still faces many problems. Its government has undergone many unexpected changes since the country won its independence in 1822. Political uncertainty continues to be a major problem. In addition, there are tremendous gaps in income between the rich and poor and between the various regions of the country. Coping with the rapid movement of people from rural areas to large cities presents many social, political, and economic challenges to the people and leaders of Brazil.

During the 1990s, Brazil's economy grew very quickly. In order to facilitate this growth, the country borrowed heavily on international

99

financial markets. It will not be easy to repay the huge debts accumulated during this period. Despite its large debts, Brazil still needs to continue to expand its industrial base in order to create new jobs for its people. The need for jobs is amplified by the fact that large numbers of young people are entering the labor force. At the same time, technological improvements in agriculture, which make it possible to replace human workers with modern machines, require that many millions of landless farm workers be retrained and given different jobs.

In the recent past, Brazil moved from the protectionist policies that began under Getúlio Vargas to an economy that welcomed foreign trade and investments during the 1990s. In the early years of the twenty-first century, however, conflicts have again arisen between supporters of free trade and protectionism. The changes in Brazil's economic structure have not been painless. The country's huge international debt has had a painful impact on many Brazilian businesses. Continued economic progress will require global economic cooperation. It will also demand a healthy local business environment and a stable, responsible government.

Another serious problem facing Brazil, one that is of special concern to the government, involves the large gaps in income and wealth between the rich and poor. Welfare programs alone cannot solve the problems of the poor. They need better education, job training, and employment opportunities in order to overcome poverty.

Within Brazil there are many differences of opinion over how the needed changes can best be brought about. These beliefs were reflected in the elections held in the fall of 2002. The election of Luiz Inacio Lula da Silva to the presidency has caused great concern among some and much hope among others. During the election campaign, "Lula," as he is called, expressed viewpoints that were radically different from those of the previous administration. Since his election, he has moderated his opinions considerably.

For Brazil to succeed, it will need to improve education and opportunities for the poor without employing radical measures that might make the rest of society les productive. The nation will need to produce both an honest and effective government. It will also have to deal with the many hurdles that have been placed upon the country by the international community—some of which have been influenced by Brazil's large international debts and some of which are related to the results of the last political election. At the same time, Brazil faces problems because of some nations' negative attitudes toward South America that are in part the result of the financial difficulties of some of Brazil's neighbors.

Despite these many challenges, there is much hope for Brazil. The country's national anthem refers to it as "A giant due to its nature . . . in its future this greatness is mirrored." If Brazil is able to overcome its problems, it will surely become the "land of the future."

Facts at a Glance

Country name	Long form: Federative Republic of Brazil
	Short form: Brazil
Nationality	Brazilian(s)
Location	Eastern tropical and subtropical South America, bordering The Atlantic Ocean
Capital city	Brasilia
Area	3,300,000 square miles (8,500,000 sq km); occupies roughly one-half of South American land mass; slightly smaller than the United States
Boundaries	Shares border with 10 South American countries: Uruguay, Argentina, and Paraguay to the south; Bolivia, Peru, and Colombia to the west; Venezuela, Guyana, Suriname, and French Guiana to the north. On the continent, only Chile and Ecuador lack a common border with Brazil. 4,655 mile (7491 km) border on Atlantic Ocean
Climate & ecosystem	Humid tropical (rainforest), seasonal wet and dry tropical (savanna) and humid subtropical (mixed forests and grassland) in the far south
Terrain	Mainly flat to rolling lowland plains in north; plateau, hills, and low mountains in the east and southeast, with highest elevations on the eastern margin; narrow, fertile Atlantic coastal plain
Elevation extremes	Pico da Neblina in the Guiana Highlands at the country's northernmost tip reaches 9,888 feet (3,014 m); lowest elevation is sea level
Natural resources	Minerals (bauxite, gemstones, gold, iron ore, manganese, nickel, petroleum, phosphates, platinum, tin, uranium), timber and forest products, water power
Natural hazards	Flooding; drought in northeast; occasional frost in south; landslides; various fish, insect transmitted diseases, and snakes
Land use	Agricultural land: 8%; urban and other use: 1%; forest, grassland, and other: 91%
Environmental issues	Deforestation of the Amazon rainforest; illegal trade in wildlife; toxic pollution resulting from mining activity; pollution of air and water, particularly in urban areas; oil spills
Population	176,000,000 (2003 est.)

Population growth rate	1.3%
Life expectancy at birth	64 years (60 males; 68 females)
Ethnic groups	European origin (Portuguese, German, Italian, Spanish, Polish), 55%; mixed white and black, 38%; black 6%; other (including Japanese and American Indian), 1%
Religion	Roman Catholic, 80%; 20% Protestant or other
Language	Portuguese (official); Spanish, English, French as second languages
Literacy	85% (2003 est.)
Independence	7 September 1822 (from Portugal)
Type of government	Federal republic
Head of state	President
Branches of government	Executive, Legislative (bicameral national congress), and Judicial
Administrative divisions	26 states and 1 federal district (Brasilia)
Voting	Voluntary age 16–18 and over 70; compulsory between 18 and 70 years of age
Currency	Real
Gross domestic product	$1.35 trillion (2002 est.)
Labor force by occupation	Services, 54%; industry, 25%; agriculture, 21%
Economy by activity	Services, 60%; industry, 33%; agriculture, 8%
Industries	Aircraft, cement, chemicals, clothing and textiles, iron ore, lumber, machinery and equipment, mining, motor vehicles
Agricultural production	Beef, citrus, coffee, cocoa, corn, rice, soybeans, sugarcane
Primary exports	($58 billion, 2001 est.); automobiles and auto parts, coffee, iron ore, manufactured goods including clothing and shoes, soybeans
Primary export partners	US 25%, Argentina 11%, Germany 9%, Japan 6%, Italy 4%
Primary imports	($58 billion, 2001 est.); Automobiles and auto parts, chemical products, electricity, machinery and equipment, petroleum
Primary import partners	US 24%, Argentina 11%, Germany 9%, Japan 6%, Italy 4%
Transportation	*Highways:* 1,242,700 miles (2,000,000 km), of which 114,854 miles (184,140 km) are paved
	Railroads: 19,337 miles (31,120 km), divided among four gauges
	Airports: 3,365
	Waterways: 31,069 miles (50,000 km)

History at a Glance

c. 35000 BC	Possible evidence of human habitation
1494 AD	Treaty of Tordesillas divided New World between Spaniards and Portuguese
1500	Portuguese explorer, Pedro Alvares Cabral, first known European to reach Brazil and claim the territory for Portugal
1532	First permanent Portuguese settlement established at Sao Vicente
1554	Jesuits establish settlement at Sao Paulo
16th-17th C	Estimated 3 to 4 million African slaves brought to Brazil, primarily to work on sugar plantations
1690s	Gold discovered in what is now Minas Gerais state
1790s	Brazil producing estimated one half of world's total gold
1820s	Coffee becomes a major Brazilian crop
1808	Portuguese king, having fled Napoleon's army in 1807, establishes seat of government in Brazil
1815	Dom Joao VI declares Brazil a kingdom equal to Portugal
1822	Son of Portuguese king declares full independence from Portugal and crowns himself Peter I, Emperor of Brazil. September 7, Brazil becomes independent country
1880s	Beginning of rubber boom era in Amazon region
1888	Slavery abolished
1889	Monarchy overthrown and federal government established.
1900	Brazil producing some 65% of world's coffee
1920s	Rubber industry begins sharp decline
1930	Revolutionary government formed by Getulio Vargas
1937	Vargas, with military support, establishes himself as dictator
1945	Vargas removed by military coup. New constitution written
1951	Vargas elected to presidency
1954	Vargas commits suicide
1960	President Juscelino Kubitschek moves capital from Rio de Janeiro to undeveloped interior site on which Brasilia was built
1966	Amazon city of Manaus made a free port in hope of further developing interior
1988	New constitution adopted, reducing presidential powers

1992   Earth Summit conference held in Rio de Janeiro

2002   Brazil wins soccer's World Cup for record 5th time

Luiz Inacia "Lula" da Silva, believed by some to be a "radical, left wing, socialist," elected president on his fourth attempt to gain the office

Further Reading

Central Intelligence Agency. *CIA-The World Factbook,* Brazil (annually updated).

Eakin, Marshall Craig. *Brazil: The Once and Future Country.* New York: St. Martin's press, 1997.

Fausto, Boris. *A Concise History of Brazil.* Cambridge, United Kingdom; Cambridge University Press, 1999.

Levine, Robert and Crocitti, John. *The Brazil Reader: History, Culture, and Politics.* Durham: Duke University press, 1999.

Perrone, Charles and Dunn, Christopher, eds. *Brazilian Popular Music and Globalization.* Gainseville: University Press of Florida, 2001.

For further information on this country, contact the Brazilian embassy at 3006 Massachusetts Avenue, NW, Washington, D.C. 20008-3634.

Index

Index

page:

8:	New Millennium Images	60:	Eraldo Peres/AP
11:	21st Century Publishing	63:	New Millennium Images
14:	New Millennium Images	66:	© Bettmann/Corbis
17:	21st Century Publishing	70:	KRT/NMI
22:	New Millennium Images	75:	KRT/NMI
25:	New Millennium Images	78:	AFP/NMI
28:	© Pierre Colombel/Corbis	80:	© Galen Rowell/Corbis
38:	© Archivo Iconografico, S.A./Corbis	85:	Dario Lopez-Mills/AP
40:	AFP/NMI	90:	New Millennium Images
47:	Renzo Gostoli/AP	97:	New Millennium Images
54:	AP/Wide World Photos	98:	AFP/NMI
58:	New Millennium Images		

Cover: New Millennium Images

About the Author

HARRY GREENBAUM is a retired professor of economics at South Dakota State University. His wife, Lillian, is native to Brazil and together they have made many trips to her homeland. Dr. Greenbaum is delighted to have the opportunity to share his interest in and love for Brazil and its people with the readers of this book.

CHARLES F. ("FRITZ") GRITZNER is Distinguished Professor of Geography at South Dakota University in Brookings. He is now in his fifth decade of college teaching and research. During his career, he has taught more than 60 different courses, spanning the fields of physical, cultural, and regional geography. In addition to his teaching, he enjoys writing, working with teachers, and sharing his love for geography with students. As consulting editor for the MODERN WORLD NATIONS series, he has a wonderful opportunity to combine each of these "hobbies." Fritz has served as both president and executive director of the National Council for Geographic Education and has received the Council's highest honor, the George J. Miller Award for Distinguished Service.